GREAT OUSE COUNTRY

Andrew Hunter Blair

ISBN   1 904136 07 9

Published by
John Nickalls Publications.
Oak Farm Bungalow, Suton, Wymondham, Norfolk, NR18 9SH.

Printed by
Geo. R. Reeve Ltd., 9-11 Town Green, Wymondham, Norfolk, NR18 0BD.

GREAT OUSE COUNTRY

Sketches of its riverside folk and history from source to mouth

Andrew Hunter Blair

To Charis

CONTENTS

Page

Index of Illustrations vi
Acknowledgements viii
Introduction ix

1   THE BEGINNING 1
The Source, George Washington, The Bishop of Durham,
The Countess of Huntingdon, Magna Carta.

2   SNAILS AND PANCAKES 8
St Guthlac, Queen Eleanor, Railways, Sir Everard Digby,
Snails, William Cowper, Pancakes.

3   MEANDERING GYVES 19
Bridges, Jonah, The Oakley Hunt, King Henry VII,
Christian Coming, Sir Lewis Dyve, Sir Samuel Luke,
A Brewery.

4   PENAL REFORM AND HANGINGS 29
Navigation, Sir John Rennie, The Grand Union Canal Link,
John Bunyan, Bedford Prison, John Howard, James Hanratty,
Glen Miller, Airships, The Danes.

5   THE SLOUGH OF DESPOND 40
More Danes, Ely Cathedral, The Slough of Despond, Nicholas
Rowe, More Breweries, A Giant, Anglian Water, A Bishop's
Palace, Stammerers, Samual Pepys, Murders.

6   "OUSE SLOWLY WINDING THROUGH
A LEVEL PLAIN" 52
Oliver Cromwell, Cowper Again, Millers and Flooding, The
RAF, A Village Philanthropist, The Gunning Sisters, Lucy Boston,
St Ivo, A Holy Well, Ghosts.

  Page

7 A RIVER FLOWS BACKWARDS   64
   The Fens, The Romans, Sir Cornelius Vermuyden, The Nine
   Tailors, Emperor Comodus, Turkey, Fish and Gutta Percha,
   Floods, Droughts.

8 THE SHIP OF THE FENS   77
   A Hermit, The Great Eastern Railway, William the Conqueror
   and Hereward the Wake, Joseph Hempsall, The Car Dyke, A
   Pumping Engine, The Lodes, St Etheldreda, Queen Adelaide.

9 RIOTS, HANGINGS, DROWNINGS AND SABOTAGE   89
   The Boat Race, Littleport Riots, Macabre Killings, A Great
   Sasse, A Water Grid, Breeches Buoy, Horatio Nelson, King John.

10 FULL CIRCLE?   101
   Vancouver, Fluvial Floods, The Greenhouse Effect, Tidal Floods,
   A Return To Primeval Conditions.

REFERENCES AND FURTHER READING.   107

INDEX OF ILLUSTRATIONS

Cover and frontispiece.
Near Tempsford
Ely Cathedral

Page

Chapter 1.
Wappenham Lodge Farm 2
Whitfield Mill 4
At Turweston Bridge 5
Water Stratford 7

Chapter 2.
Buckingham Riverside 9
"The Iron Trunk" 12
Lathbury Church 14
Tyringham Bridge 16
Olney ..... 18 and colour i

Chapter 3.
Newton Blossomville 20
Turvey Bridge 21
Harrold Bridge 22
Felmersham Bridge 24
Holy Well at Stevington ..... 25 and colour ii
Bromham Bridge 26

Chapter 4.
Kempston, the Limit of Navigation 30
The River Front at Bedford 32
Bedford County Court House ..... 35 and colour iv
Cardington Hangers 36
Howard's House ..... 37 and colour v
Willington Dovecote 39

Chapter 5.
Great Barford Bridge 41
The Slough of Despond 43
The Priory Brewery, St Neots ..... 44 and colour iii
St Neots River Front 45
Godmanchester 48
Huntingdon Bridge 50

	Page
Chapter 6.	
Oliver Cromwell	53
Houghton Mill	56
The Manor House, Hemingford Grey	58 and colour vi
St James Church, Hemingford Grey	59
St Ives Bridge	61
Holywell	62
Chapter 7.	
Brownshill Staunch	65
A Fenland Scene	67
The Old Bedford River in Flood	71
The Hundred Foot or New Bedford River in Summer	72
Bluntisham Church	73
Bury Fen in the Summer	74 and colour viii
Chapter 8.	
Hermitage Lock	78
On the Old West River	79
Aldreth Causeway	80
The Old West River from Aldreth High Bridge	81 and colour vii
Stretham Old Engine	83
A Ship of the Fens	85
Chapter 9.	
Queen Adelaide Straight	90 and colour viii
"Quite exciting to see a cow"	92
Below Denver Sluice	94
Wiggenhall St Mary Magdalen	96
Wiggenhall St Peter	97
The Guildhall, King's Lynn	99
Chapter 10.	
George Vancouver at the Customs House	102
The Mouth	104
Flood Marks	105

ACKNOWLEDGEMENTS

Grateful acknowledgement is made to the authors of the publications listed under References and Further Reading, which have been used extensively when researching this book. These authors include those who have prepared numerous town, village, church, and conservation guides. The author would also like to thank all those who have given additional information, including The Charles Wells Brewery, National Power, The Kier Group, Anglian Water, The Environment Agency, The Middle Level Commissioners, The Cam Conservancy, The Fens Tourism Group, The Great Ouse Boating Association, The Borough Council of King's Lynn and West Norfolk, Cambridgeshire County Council Libraries and Information Service, Tourist Information Centres, Conservation Bodies, museum staff, as well as those the author met in churches, at marinas, on footpaths, on boats, and at locks.

The maps have been reproduced from the
1999 Explorer 191, Banbury, Bicester & Chipping Norton, 1:25,000,
1998 Explorer 192, Buckingham & Milton Keynes, 1:25,000,
1999 Explorer 207, Newport Pagnell & Northampton South, 1:25,000,
1999 Explorer 208, Bedford & St Neots, 1:25,000,
1999 Explorer 225, Huntingdon & St Ives, 1:25,000,
1999 Explorer 228, March & Ely, 1:25,000,
1999 Explorer 236, King's Lynn, Downham Market & Swaffham, 1:25,000,
1999 Explorer 249, Spalding and Holbeach, 1:25,000,
Ordnance Survey maps by permission of Ordnance Survey on behalf of the Controller of Her Majesty's Stationery Office, © Crown Copyright MC 100036267.

The author particularly acknowledges the help and encouragement given by Archie Buchanan Esq., the agreement by William Wilson Esq. of Imray Laurie Norie and Wilson to the publication of this book which contains some material written previously by the author and published by Imray, and the assistance of Bob Burn-Murdoch of the Norris Library and Museum, St Ives. Special thanks are given to Steve Benz Esq., of S. B. Publications who enabled the publication of this book.

Olney – See Chapter Two

Holy Well at Stevington – See Chapter 3

The Priory Brewery, St Neots – See Chapter 5

Bedford County Court House – See Chapter 4

Howard's House – See Chapter 4

The Manor House, Hemingford Grey – See Chapter 6

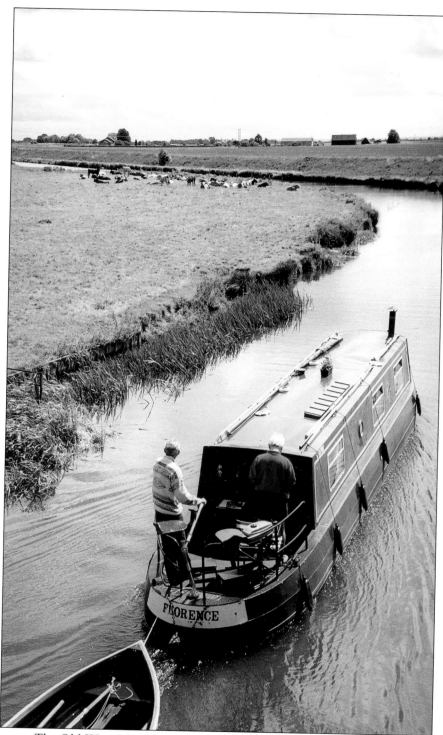

The Old West River from Aldreth High Bridge – See Chapter 8

Bury Fen in the Summer – See Chapter 7

Queen Adelaide Straight – See Chapter 9

INTRODUCTION

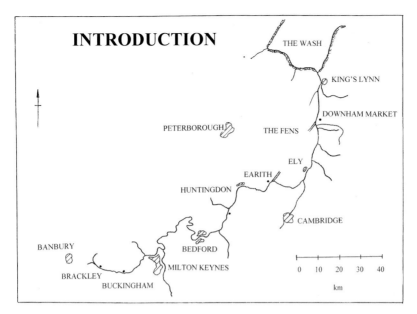

The Ouse is a slow moving river. There is one in Yorkshire, one in Sussex, a Little one in Norfolk and a Great one in the Midlands and East Anglia. It rises near Brackley in Northamptonshire and passes through Buckinghamshire, Bedfordshire, Huntingdonshire, Cambridgeshire, and Norfolk during its 260km journey to the sea at King's Lynn. It is the common thread between not only village, town, city and county, but also between the past, present and future, fact and fiction, the famous and the infamous, and the well known and the obscure.

It is a river of great contrasts. In its upper reaches it is an ancient river meandering in a wide flood plain. In its lower reaches it is artificial and straight, lying between high flood banks. It has suffered from droughts and catastrophic floods with loss of life. It has been influenced by the Romans, the Dutch and the British. It influenced the poets Nicholas Rowe and William Cowper and the writers John Bunyan, Dorothy Sayers and Lucy Boston. The Danes, the English, William the Conqueror and Hereward the Wake fought over its waters; St Neot, St Ivo and St Etheldreda brought peace. Beside it, Mary and Elizabeth Gunning loved the Earl of Coventry, the Duke of Hamilton and the Duke of Argyle, but Mary Weems was murdered by her husband. In Huntingdon, Oliver Cromwell was born; in Bedford, James Hanratty was hung. Pancakes are raced beside it and rowers race on it.

A unique and fascinating picture of the characters and characteristics of the River Great Ouse emerges, reflected through some of the places, events and lives, all of which, in one way or another, have this Great River in common.

Andrew Hunter Blair is a chartered civil engineer, who was educated at Rugby School and Queen's University, Belfast, where he gained his B.Sc. and M.Sc. Following a short spell with the Great Ouse River Board in Cambridge, he worked for nine years at the Water Research Association/Centre at Medmenham near Henley on Thames, where he pioneered work on the quality and quantity of underground water. During this period he prepared and presented many papers at both national and international conferences. Returning to East Anglia in 1974, he joined Anglian Water headquarters where he worked on the fluvial and tidal aspects of water management. On its formation, he continued this work within the National Rivers Authority at its Anglian Region headquarters in Peterborough. He retired from his post as Regional Co-ordinator in December 1993 after which he undertook consultancy work for Sir William Halcrow and Partners and the Middle Level Commissioners.

Having spent most of his working life in East Anglia, he has grown to know its rivers, particularly the River Great Ouse and those in the Fens. This knowledge has been demonstrated in two practical publications popular with all river users, particularly navigators: The River Great Ouse and its Tributaries; A guide for river users and The Middle Level; A map and commentary on the Fenland Waterways both published in 2000 by Imray Laurie Norie and Wilson of St Ives in Cambridgeshire.

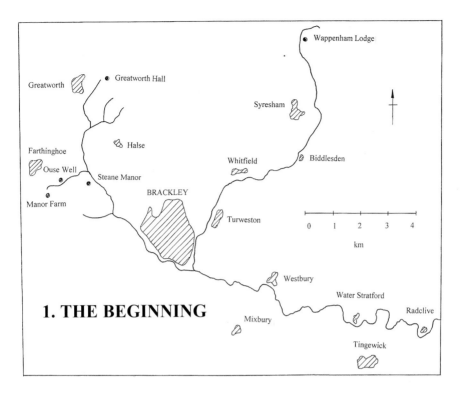

1. THE BEGINNING

The north and west of Northamptonshire form the "watershed" of England. In the north, the River Welland flowing east to Spalding and the Wash, is the boundary between Northamptonshire, and Leicestershire and Rutland; the River Nene rises near Daventry and flows east through Peterborough and Wisbech to the Wash; west of Naseby, the River Avon rises and flows south west between Warwick and Leamington Spa to the River Severn; the River Leam flows north and then west to Leamington Spa and thence to the Rivers Avon and Severn; the River Cherwell rises at Charwelton, near Daventry and flows south west to the Thames; the longest river leaving the county, the River Great Ouse rises near Brackley and flows east to King's Lynn.

By the time it passes Brackley, it is a small river; a "natural stream of water flowing in a channel to the sea". But where is its source, its "point of origin or issue"? Is it to the west of Brackley near Farthinghoe Manor Farm, north west of Brackley near Greatworth Hall or north east of Brackley near Wappenham Lodge Farm?

Traditionalists favour the brooks and springs which rise near Farthinghoe, on the watershed between the Ouse and Thames valleys, and flow through a spot called Ouse Well. This source is the most south west and therefore, as the crow flies, the furthest from the mouth of the river, at King's

1

Lynn, some 140km to the north west. On the other hand the brook which rises near Greatworth is longer than the Farthinghoe branch. It was said that a spring in the cellar of the former Greatworth Manor divided in two; one stream flowed west to Oxford via the Cherwell, the other flowed east via Ouse Well forming the River Great Ouse. In a somewhat tenuous argument, this well enabled Oxford and Cambridge to be linked directly by water, the rivers Cherwell, Great Ouse and Cam being the relevant watercourses. These two brooks from Farthinghoe and Greatworth combine near Steane Manor and flow to the south of Brackley where they meet another brook that rose near Wappenham.

Recognised by the Ordnance Survey as the River Great Ouse, the Wappenham brook is significantly longer than the Greatford brook and is therefore, "as the fish swims", the furthest from the sea. By this definition the source of the River Great Ouse is on the watershed between the Ouse and Tove valleys, about 600m north east of Wappenham Lodge Farm, 150m above sea level, and about 260km from its mouth in the Wash.

Returning to Greatworth, it was here, in the late 16th century and early 17th century, that two sisters, Amy and Dorothy Pargiter, became the second wives of two brothers, Lawrence and John Washington from the small village of Sulgrave just to the north of Greatworth. Soon after their marriages, they were said to have moved to Brington, near Althorpe. Regardless of whether they actually lived there, they are buried in Brington church, also the resting place of early members of the Spencer family. In all three villages the Washington coat of arms comprising three stars above two stripes are in evidence. It is thought that this crest was the basis of the American Stars and Stripes, through George Washington, the first president of the United States of America and, the great great great grandson of Lawrence Washington.

The Greatworth and Farthinghoe streams meet at Steane (Stene). Whilst there is little trace of the village which was destroyed by the Black Death, parts of its 17th century manor house remain, incorporated into a farmhouse. The manor itself dates back to the 15th century when it was first given to Sir Thomas Bray by Henry VII in return for Thomas' loyalty and for finding the crown of England in a thorn tree at Bosworth Field in 1485. In the early 17th century the manor passed through marriage to Sir Thomas Crew(e) (1565-1634), speaker of the House of Commons, MP for Northampton and a member of the Ecclesiastical Commission. It was he who built the private chapel there in c1620 with box pews and a double-decker pulpit. His descendant, Nathaniel Crew (1633-1721), the third Baron Crew of Stene, was born and died at the manor. He became the Bishop of Oxford (1671) and the Bishop of Durham (1674) and thus possibly the first both spiritual and temporal peer in the country. He also held the Deanery of the Chapel Royal in Windsor from whence he brought to Stene, trophies including altar vestments, a pulpit, a reading desk and bibles and prayer books used by both Charles II and William III. In the family monument he is depicted lying beside his second wife, who had predeceased him. After her death the Bishop used to sit beside her monument on top of which was a skull. He became so depressed at the sight of this that he had it changed to a bunch of grapes.

Although Wappenham itself is actually outside the Great Ouse catchment, it is in the catchment of the River Tove which in turn flows into the Great Ouse near Stony Stratford. In the parish is the site of the 16th century Astwell Castle, one of three early fortified manors in the county. It is believed to be the birth place in 1701 of Selina Hastings, Countess of Huntingdon. The wife of the ninth Earl of Huntingdon, Theophilus Hastings, she was a close friend of the Wesleys, supported itinerant lay preachers, set up churches and chapels which were registered as Dissenting Meeting Houses, and founded the religious sect known as Lady Huntingdon's Connection.

The brook flows south from Wappenham Lodge through Syresham (Northamptonshire) where in the Wesleyan chapel there is a memorial:

In memory of John Kurde, shoemaker, the Syresham martyr,
burned at the stake in defence of truth, 1557.
Tell ye your children of it, and let your children tell their children
and their children another generation.

3

to Biddlesden, (Buckinghamshire) in whose park is the site of a former Cistercian abbey. It was from here after its dissolution that a marble altar slab was removed and let down into the floor of the nave of Wappenham church. It is the tomb stone of Sir Thomas Billing (d c1481), chief justice of Edward IV, and his wife Katherine (d c1479).

The brook now flows south west past the unspoilt stone village of Whitfield and Turweston with its Norman church, to join the Greatford/Farthinghoe brook just to the south east of Brackley, so becoming an established river.

In the 12th/13th century, two hospitals were founded in Brackley, one, of which no trace remains, was dedicated to St Leonard for the relief of lepers. The other, the Hospital of St James and St John was founded by Robert de Burn, Earl of Leicester. Originally it had resident brothers, but it was refounded in 1423 for travellers and then in 1484 sold to William of Waynflete (1395?-1486) who handed it to his Oxford foundation, Magdalen College. During the plague in Oxford it was used as a safe haven for scholars and fellows. At the Dissolution of the Monasteries it became Magdalen College School. The original hospital chapel still survives, albeit much restored, and must be one of the oldest school chapels in England. The Earl of Leicester's heart was buried in this chapel and during some late 19th century restoration, a workman found an "old bit of leather" in a lead casket; it was just thrown away!

Brackley became of importance during the Middle Ages, during the build up to the Magna Carta and Runnymead, when c1215, Barons assembled at Brackley Castle before sending their demands to King John in Oxford. They chose as their leader, Robert Fitzwalter, "Marshall of the Army of God and of the Holy Church". King John refused to meet their demands and it was left to Simon de Montfort to try to settle their differences with Henry III.

After the reformation the town's importance diminished until the early 18th century when it had a reputation for harbouring thieves and vagrants.

Brackley Breed
Better to hang than feed

One kilometre below the confluence of the two brooks, between Brackley and Westbury, near the spot where the former Great Central Railway from Marylebone to Rugby, Sheffield and Manchester crossed the River Great Ouse, the river is at the junction of three counties, Northamptonshire, Oxfordshire and Buckinghamshire. Indeed, for the next 5km or so it in effect forms the boundary between Oxfordshire to the south and Buckinghamshire to the north. Since rivers are perhaps the oldest form of natural boundary, they have long been adopted as administrative boundaries. One of the earliest examples of the Great Ouse forming such a boundary is the stretch between the Watling Street crossing and Bedford. This was the stretch which, in a treaty drawn up between Alfred and Guthrum in c890, was the boundary between the Kingdom of Mercia and the Danelaw. Whilst it is pure speculation, the fact that three counties have a common point on the river might suggest that this site was once of some significance, perhaps an ancient river crossing.

Whilst there can be speculation about a river crossing at the three counties junction, there can be no doubt that there was a major river crossing at Water Stratford. It is here that the Roman road from Winchester and Bicester to Towcester via Stowe crossed the river and thus gave the village its first name of Streetford. In the small parish church of St Giles, with its Norman doorways is a black marble monument to Mary Franckyshe who died in 1630 during the delivery of her tenth child. Aged only 32, she is depicted lying in bed surrounded by her nine sons and daughters with her husband standing at the foot of her bed.

Forty four years later the church was to become well known through its somewhat eccentric vicar John Mason. He attracted many people to this little church through his preaching and belief that the millennium was about to take place and that the saviour would make his second Advent. Unfortunately, he did not live to see if his prophesy would come true as, during a night of celebrations he was struck dumb and died. His followers however were convinced the he, the vicar, would also rise up on the third day. Some had been so intoxicated by his preaching that they swore they had seen him resurrected. To allay this belief, the new vicar had the grave opened and the body displayed. Despite this irrefutable proof, the sect continued with its belief until about 1740.

2. SNAILS AND PANCAKES

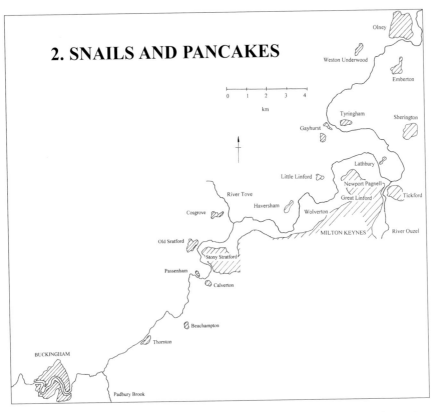

At Water Stratford, the Oxfordshire and Buckinghamshire boundary leaves the river and follows the line of the Roman road to the south west. Now totally in Buckinghamshire, the river meanders past Tingewick Mill and round Radclive to Buckingham, the town which gave its name to the county, but which is not the county town. Buckingham first came to prominence in about 886 when Alfred the Great declared it to be the county town. About 30 years later Edward the Elder, during his advance against the Danes, visited the town and stayed there with his army for about four weeks, during which time he constructed fortifications on each side of the river. After the Norman Conquest, the manor passed to Walter Giffard, who was created the first Earl of Buckingham in 1070, and whose descendants would hold the manor until the execution in 1521 of Edward Stafford, the third Duke of Buckingham, by Henry VIII. Thus ended the first creation of the Dukes of Buckingham; the title was to be re-established 70 years later.

The Giffard family bequeathed their family crest of a golden chained swan to the town. Originally the crest of Eleanor de Bohun, it was later to be adopted as the county crest. The family also built another castle, which in the later part of the 18th century was cleared to make way for the church of St Peter and St Paul. Its construction was funded by the Temple family from

Stowe who had been restoring the town following a disastrous fire in 1725, which had destroyed over one third of the town's houses, and who wished it to form a focus of their view from Stowe House. Initially an ugly church, it was rebuilt in 1862 by the architect Sir Gilbert Scott (1811-1878), who had been born a few kilometres to the south at Gawcott, where his father had been vicar. Sir Gilbert, although well known for his ecclesiastical restorations and rebuildings, is perhaps best known for his design of St Pancras Station and Hotel.

Near the church are St Rumbold's Street and Well Street. St Rumbold was a legendary Saxon baby who lived for three days. After his baptism in 621, he delivered a long sermon and then promptly died. His body spent a year at Kings Sutton, his birth place and two years at Brackley, before being returned forever to Buckingham. His body, together with a nearby sacred well, formed the centre of a miracle working cult which continued until the reformation.

Not only was Henry VIII responsible for the third Duke of Buckingham's execution, probably on trumped up charges, but he also removed the assizes to Aylesbury, the county town which already had the county assize courts. There they remained until the summer assizes were returned in 1708 when the town's fortunes were improving. To celebrate their return, Lord Cobham built for the town in 1748, a gaol and gaoler's house in the style of a mock castle.

Buckingham lay on a branch of the London and North Western Railway and on its own link to the Grand Union Canal, the 17km Buckingham Arm. Running close too and roughly parallel with the river, it comprised of two separate concerns, the narrow Buckingham Arm and the wider Old Stratford Cut. Both parts are now partly derelict and disused.

Between Maids Morton Mill and the late 18th century Thornborough Mill, the Great Ouse is joined from the south by its first tributary of any significance, the Padbury Brook or the Twins. The brook is crossed by Thornborough Bridge, the only 14th century bridge in the county. Now bypassed by a modern bridge, the ancient three metres wide bridge comprises of six arches, three of which are pointed and ribbed. Close to the bridge are the Thornborough Mounds, two Roman burial mounds attributed to Aulus Plautus who lost two generals nearby. In 1839 one was opened by the Duke of Buckingham and two bronze jugs, a bronze lamp and pottery indicative of the late 2nd century were discovered.

After passing the small village of Thornton, the river once again becomes a boundary, this time between Northamptonshire to the north and Buckinghamshire to the south. The churches of Thornton and Beachampton both contain memorials of distinction. In Thornton, the rebuilt church of St Michael and All Angels contains an exceptionally good brass memorial depicting Robert Ingylton (1472), his three wives and their 16 kneeling children below, as well as a mid 15th century alabaster of one John Barton and his wife. At Beachampton, the church, dating from the 14th century and again largely rebuilt, contains a striking memorial to Sir Simon Benet (d1682) of Beachampton Hall, depicted with a wig and lace fronted shirt. He was a benefactor to University College, Oxford, through which, it is said, the monument was erected in c1760. However, judging by the style and clothes, the bust itself may be about 100 years older.

Passenham lies across the border in Northamptonshire and its church of St Guthlac, dates from the 12th century. St Guthlac (c663-714) of Saxon royal descent, became a hermit and lived in the Fens where ague and malaria were rife and where the land was "oft-times clouded with moist and dark vapours". It is not inconceivable that water which flowed past Passenham, might in some small measure have found its way past Crowland Abbey, built c716 by Ethelbald, King of Mercia over the Saint's shrine. The church has survived the ravishes of over zealous restoration, the last major work being carried out in 1626 by Sir Robert Banastre, a courtier to James I and Charles I, allegedly a bit of a bounder and villain, and who "featured in local ghost stories". The building and its furniture thus retain the atmosphere of an early 17th century church.

After passing the site of a ford which joined Passenham with Calverton, the river forms yet another boundary, albeit slowly being eroded, around the western and northern fringes of Milton Keynes. It takes its name from the small village of Milton Keynes built on the east bank of the River Ouzel, the manor of which was owned by the Keynes family in the 13th century. Whilst it may be thought in terms of a grid of roads, cycle-ways and roundabouts, with a landscape populated with concrete cows, there is a history to the ancient villages which are now subsumed in this conurbation.

First are the Stratfords, Old Stratford in Northamptonshire and Stony Stratford in Buckinghamshire. The early Roman settlement was on the north bank, originally near Cosgrove, but which by the end of the 13th century had moved west towards Old Stratford. The Stratfords are linked by Watling Street, a Roman Road running between London and Chester. Its name is derived from people called Waeclingas; nothing is known of them or of their circumstances. Since the early 19th century, the road has become associated with Thomas Telford as it formed the basis for his London to Holyhead Road, the modern A5.

In 1290, the body of King Edward I's wife, Queen Eleanor of Castille, rested at Stony Stratford for one night during her funeral procession from Nottinghamshire to London. To commemorate the journey, "Eleanor Crosses" were erected at the halting places and accordingly one was placed in the High Street, where it remained until its destruction in 1646. Given the nature of the road and its strategic river crossing, there must have been many more important personages who passed on their way to or from London. Another such royal instance concerns Edward IV, married to Lady Elizabeth Woodville in 1464. He stayed many times at the since destroyed Guildhouse. After his death in 1483, his heir, Prince Edward, stayed a night at Stony Stratford before proceeding to London to join his brother, unexpectedly, in the Tower of London.

> *Last night, I hear, they lay at Stony-Stratford;*
> *and at Northampton they rest tonight:*
> *Tomorrow or the next day they will be here.*
>
> *Richard III*

During the 15th and 16th century the town became well known for the number of inns. Despite disastrous fires in 1736, when over 200 houses were destroyed, and 1742, at least two remain, next door to each other; the Cock and the Bull. Here gossip was exchanged, each inn vying with the other, giving rise to the expression "a Cock and Bull story".

In 1927 Stony Stratford was incorporated into the mid Victorian railway town of Wolverton. The town was not however a railway town first. Before the arrival of the railway it had been a canal town lying on the Grand Union Canal which was carried across the River Great Ouse towards Cosgrove in an aqueduct, completed in 1811 and known as "The Iron Trunk". Shortly below the aqueduct, the river is joined from the north by the next tributary, the River Tove. This now forms the Northamptonshire and Buckinghamshire county boundary.

Following the arrival of the London and North Western (later London, Midland and Scottish) railway line in the late 1830s, and the inauguration of the London to Birmingham railway in 1838, rows of small terrace houses were built on a symmetrical grid for the workers of the railway company's carriage and locomotive works. Whilst the locomotive works were removed to Crewe in the 1870s, the carriage works expanded and flourished until the 1950s, after which many of the factory sites were sold.

Besides the carriage works, engineers were taught rail traffic control. When the line was clear, they were taught to stand beside the track absolutely straight up and still. If the line was blocked or there was another danger then they were to wave a red flag and when the train passed, bring it smartly to the shoulder like a salute.

Wolverton had in its turn engulfed the old villages of New Bradwell and Stantonbury. New Bradwell was another railway workers' village on the east side of the tracks. Here between 1854 and 1861, were built 187 small two storey red brick terrace houses for the workers and 17 three storey "pavilion" houses for the foremen. Most were demolished in 1974 and replaced by new terraces. Stantonbury had much earlier origins as a Romano British settlement of some four houses built within a bend of the river. Its church of St Peter, isolated on the river bank for hundreds of years and now in ruins, was founded in 950. Its religious affairs were removed to New Bradwell parish church of St James in 1909. An earlier attempt to remove these affairs resulted in the disconcerting invalidation of over 1000 local marriages!

At the eastern edge of Milton Keynes, the river flows between Great and Little Linford. In Great Linford, the almshouses and school were built between 1683 and 1704 by Sir William Pritchard (1632?-1705), Lord Mayor of London, MP for the city of London, and President of St Bartholomew's Hospital. His death is recorded on a tablet in the 13th and early 14th century church of St Andrew. In 1590, its rector was Richard Napier (or Napper), (1559-1634). Not only was he licensed to practise medicine but he was an astrologer. Consequently he was regarded by some as a bit of a wizard and magician, apparently able to converse with the angel Raphael and to prophesy the future. According to legend he made his knees perfectly hard by so much kneeling in prayer.

Between New Bradwell and the Linfords, much of the river valley has been exploited for gravel, following which "restoration" for leisure facilities or nature reserves has taken place. Some of the workings contributed to the building of the M1 motorway which crosses the river downstream from Great Linford and here runs roughly parallel to Watling Street, the Grand Union Canal and the railway line in a corridor some 7km wide. The motorway effectively separates Milton Keynes from Newport Pagnell.

However, before it reaches the old town of Newport Pagnell the river passes the small riverside village of Lathbury whose church of All Saints is of Norman origin and where the first Lathbury House was built in 1604 by Sir William Andrewes. His son, Sir Henry, was the father of six children, five of whom died in infancy; the sixth, Margaret, died aged only 14 from a cold caught whilst walking late one evening in the garden. The property passed to Miss Elizabeth Brown, a cousin of Margaret, who married aged 16, Thomas Lord Leigh of Stoneleigh (Warwickshire). The marriage was not a happy one. Despite the efforts of Charles I to put things right, they were separated in 1676 and Elizabeth died two years later. By all accounts she was a beautiful woman and she was portrayed by Sir Peter Lely as a shepherdess.

In 1744 the estate passed to Mrs Symes, the third daughter of another Henry Andrewes, who also had had an unfortunate marriage and was separated from her husband. She was a staunch Jacobite with a sense of duty mixed with humour. When the Duke of Cumberland was marching south to oppose Charles Edward, the Young Pretender, he divided his army; one half marched down Watling Street to cross the Ouse at Stony Stratford, the other half went to Newport Pagnell to cross the Ouse at Lathbury. This crossing was known to be dangerous when the river was in flood and the owners of the Lathbury Estate built a private bridge, with gates, available to the public for a fee of 5/- when the river was unsafe. Such was the case when the Duke wanted to cross the river and when he requested the keys from Mrs Symes, he was told she was in London, with the said keys. She was actually in the house enjoying his discomfort, however the Duke had the last laugh as after two hours he broke down the gates, his troops having destroyed most of the trees and hedges of the park. She died in 1778 as "Elizabeth, Lady Leigh, Baroness of Stonly", shortly before the Manor House was rebuilt as Lathbury Park in 1801.

In total contrast, the church contains the ashes of Baron Augustus Uthwatt of Lathbury, (1879-1949). Knighted in 1941, he was a judge and in 1941 was the chairman of the Committee on Compensation and Betterment. Round the outside edge of a large meander the river passes Newport Pagnell and Tickford.

Newport Pagnell has been a great lace making town, home to William Cowley's parchment works, one of only two such works in the country, Salmon's stage coach works and David Brown's Aston Martin car factory. It was formerly a Saxon town lying on the corner of the junction of the Rivers Ouse and Ouzel, and derives its second name from Sir Fulke Paganel (d1182) Baron of Hambie in Normandy, who had inherited the manor through his marriage to the only daughter of William Fitz Ansculf. He and his descendants built Pagnell's Castle, of which only a mound remains, at the apex of the junction of the rivers.

It was an important town in the Civil War because its occupation in 1643 by the Royalists, led by Sir Lewis Dyve, threatened the Parliamentary links with the north. In October 1643, the Earl of Essex and Sir Samuel Luke rode against the town which Sir Lewis abandoned without a fight. Sir Samuel was appointed Governor and during this time it was said that he was a cautious man who never went out at night and rode a horse whose shoes were reversed to confound his pursuers. Amongst those who served with Sir Samuel, as pressed men, were John Bunyan and the eldest son of Oliver Cromwell. Meanwhile George Fox (1624-1691), founder of the Society of Friends, stayed in a local inn. Sir Samuel's governorship came to an end with the Battle of Naseby. Sir Lewis and Sir Samuel had been long time enemies and the river was again to act as a boundary, this time between their estates, respectively at Bromham and Cople, both in Bedfordshire.

Across the River Ouzel, Sir Fulke founded Tickford Abbey. Initially this was a Cluniac priory and cell of the monastery of St Martin in Tours, before being re-established in the 14th century as a cell to Holy Trinity, York. The abbey continued in use until Cardinal Wolsey appropriated its funds for works which he carried out jointly with Sir Christopher Wren in Oxford. A little upstream from Tickford on the Ouzel is the oldest (1810) cast iron bridge in the country in daily use.

Meandering north under the stone 18th century Sherington Bridge the river passes Sherington, whose parish church of St Laud (or Lo) is unusual in that it is the only church in the country dedicated to this little known 6th century French Bishop, and turns west towards Tyringham. There is no village here but the Hall is architecturally important. It was designed by Sir John Soane (1753-1837) and built in the 1970s, possibly on the site of a Saxon manor, for William Praed, a banker and the first chairman of the Grand Junction Canal Company. Whilst the Hall was drastically altered in the early 1900s, the original massive grey stone front and high sweeping bridge over the Ouse remain. Although not particularly attractive by present day standards, at the time they were built, the exacting design was daring and without precedent.

On the other side of the river is Gayhurst. Although it is a small village with only a handful of cottages, the Tudor Gayhurst House is one of the most historic manor houses in the county if not the country. The manor was first granted by William the Conqueror to his half brother Odo, Bishop of Bayeux. It then passed to tenant Ralph de Nowers, whose family was to remain there for the next 300 years until 1408, when it passed through the female line to Sir Robert Neville. In c1580 it was given to Sir Francis Drake on his return from his round the world voyage. He immediately sold it to William Mulsoe who started building the present house in 1597. As he had no male heirs, the estate passed to his son-in-law Sir Everard Digby (1578-1606) who completed the rebuilding.

Sir Everard was a friend of Robert Catesby, who lived in Ashby St Ledgers, the other side of Northampton. It was in these two homes that the Gunpowder Plot was hatched. After its failure, Sir Everard gave himself up in an unsuccessful attempt to save his life. In the event he was arrested, tried, convicted, hung, drawn and quartered, and his remains were displayed on Tower Hill.

Sir Everard's sons, Sir William and Sir Kenelm Digby, inherited the estate. Sir Kenelm (1603-1665), who had been born in the house, was a Royalist, an author, a naval commander, a diplomat, a man of learning and an early Member of the Royal Society. He claimed to have discovered "a sympathetic powder" for the care of wounds; it was of no medicinal value! It is also said that on his return from France he introduced French edible

16

snails (*Helix Pomatia*) to Gayhurst as a cure for his wife's consumption. Descendants of these pale snails can still be found on the estate. Both Sir Kenelm, described by Sir Thomas Browne as "the Ornament of England" and his wife Venetia Anastasia had their portraits painted by their friend Vandyck. "I know of no persons who are painted in a greater variety of forms and places than this illustrious pair, possibly because they are the finest subjects of the times". Not a bad reputation for the son and daughter-in-law of the executed Sir Everard!

In 1704, the two granddaughters of Sir Kenelm sold the estate to George Wright, son of Sir Nathan Wright (1654-1721), judge and Lord Keeper of the Great Seal to Queen Anne. The parish church of St Peter, built in Wren style c 1728, on the site of an ancient church, contains an exceptionally fine baroque style monument, attributed to Louis Roubiliac (1705-1762), of Sir Nathan in his robes, standing next to his son George.

Leaving Gayhurst, as the river flows downstream past Weston Underwood to Olney and Huntingdon, so its greatest poet, William Cowper, moved upstream from Huntingdon, to Olney and Weston Underwood. Before finally leaving "his" river for Norfolk, he lived in Weston Underwood, which he described "as the loveliest in England", with his companion Mrs Unwin, in Weston Lodge, a late 17th century stone cottage, close to his friends the Throckmortons of Weston Lodge. Whilst the house was destroyed in 1826, Cowper's "Wilderness" remains, but as a zoo and tropical bird garden.

Before moving to Weston Underwood, William Cowper had lived in Olney for 19 years after his arrival from Huntingdon, with his companion Mrs Unwin, in 1767 to convalesce from an illness and an attempted suicide. Their friendship had started in Huntingdon, when Mrs Unwin took William in as a lodger. Widowed just before their move to Olney, she had planned to marry William in 1772, however this did not come about due to his insanity. The mid Georgian house in the Market Square in which they lived, is now the Cowper Museum.

William became very friendly with the curate John Newton (1725-1807) and it was in the summer house of the vicarage that William wrote John Gilpin. John Newton had had a very varied career. He went to sea prior to a planned trip to the West Indies to manage a sugar plantation. Just before his departure, he had fallen in love with his 14 year old sweetheart, Mary Catlett. Because he thought that in his absence she might marry someone else, he jumped ship, only to be taken by the Press Gang to serve in HMS Harwich. Once again he deserted, only this time to be arrested, put in irons and given the "Cat O' Ninetails". When he was eventually discharged he joined a slave trader with whom he worked for several years. Ill health followed and he took a shore job in Liverpool as Tide Surveyor. Soon, however, now married to Mary, he became more and more religious and in 1764 he was appointed curate in charge of Olney for Moses Browne of Lincolnshire. An extra gallery had to be built in the parish church of St Peter and St Paul to accommodate all those who came to listen to the former slave trader turned preacher.

Just before he left Olney in 1780 for London, he and William wrote over 300 hymns, known as the Olney Hymns. These were not the only hymns to be associated with Olney. "The Father of English Church Music", Henry John Gauntlett (1805-1876), was, as a child, organist at Olney. Not only did he become a very famous organist, playing the organ at the first performance of *Elijah* in Birmingham, but he is credited with composing over 10,000 new hymn tunes.

(See colour section for larger photo)

Olney is a small attractive town with a long High Street, virtually uninterrupted by any side streets, providing an almost unbroken line of Georgian houses built or rebuilt after a mid 18th century fire. Cowper did not particularly care for the town. Although he said it was not actually unpleasant, he described it as being inhabited "chiefly by the half starved and ragged of the earth", where "occurrences here are about as rare as cucumbers at Christmas". There is, however, one famous "occurrence" reputedly started in 1445, namely the Shrove Tuesday Pancake Race. Apart from a short gap during the Second World War, it has been run every year. It is open only to housewives, who have to cook their own pancakes and then race through the town to the church, tossing them at least three times on the way. The churchwardens, dressed according to fashion in the Napoleonic War, act as officials and the winner is given a kiss by the bell ringer and a silver cup. After the race there is a church service and the frying pans are stacked around the font. Since 1950 a similar race has taken place in Liberal in Kansas and the Olney race has now become somewhat of an Anglo-American event.

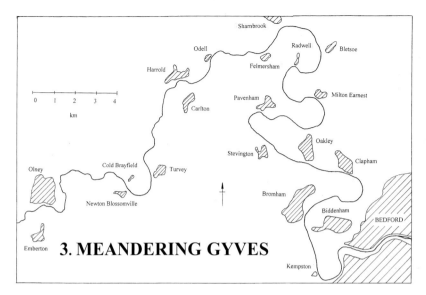

3. MEANDERING GYVES

As the river leaves the former lace making town of Olney, it flows under Olney Bridge. Dating from the 17th century, a part was reputedly built 100 years later by two friends who lived on opposite sides of the river, Sir Robert Throckmorton of Weston Underwood and William Lowndes of Astwood Bury. During times of flood they were unable to visit each other and so they built an extension over the floodplain, Sir Robert providing the materials and William the labour.

> *Ouse having Olney past, as she were waxed mad,*
> *From her first staider course immediately doth gad,*
> *And in meandering gyves doth whirl herself about,*
> *That, this way, here and there, back, forwards, in and out;*
> *And like a wanton girl, oft doubting in her gait,*
> *In labyrinth-like turns and twistings intricate,*
> *Thro' those rich fields doth run.*

The first of these meanders takes the Ouse north past Olney, now on the west bank and Clifton Reynes to the east. In the Reynes Chapel of the church of St Mary, perched on a bluff overlooking the river, are two early 14th century oak memorials to Thomas Reynes and his wife and to Ralph Reynes, and a late 14th century memorial to Thomas Reynes III and his dog Bo. Running north from Clifton Reynes, an ancient track, possibly Roman, crosses the river at Lavendon Mill and continues north past Lavendon Grange. This was built c1625 on the site of a Premonstratensian (Norbertine) abbey founded by John de Bedun in c1154. Suppressed in the 16th century, only traces now remain.

Shortly after passing between the small villages of Cold Brayfeld on the north bank and Newton Blossomville on the south, the River Great Ouse becomes a boundary again, this time between Buckinghamshire to the west and Bedfordshire to the east. As it twists and turns through Bedfordshire, like a many coiled snake, it is not surprising that of 123 ancient parishes, all but six were joined to the river or one of its tributaries. On its way to Bedford, the river flows first north and then east after which a series of six large meanders, each of which turns through 180°, drop the river generally southwards before its final easterly run to the county town. In so doing it passes 17 Bedfordshire villages, the first of which is Turvey, 9km from Bedford as the crow flies; 36km as the fish swims. The ancient road from London to Bedford continues north west through five of these villages crossing the river twice, at Stafford Bridge Oakley, and Harrold Bridge. The railway line from Leicester to Bedford crosses the river six times on long viaducts.

A particular feature of this stretch of river are its ancient bridges and Turvey Bridge, mentioned first in 1138, is no exception. First built with 16 arches, it was remodelled and repaired in 1795 and again in 1825. Half in Buckinghamshire and half in Bedfordshire, it was declared a Bedford County bridge in 1881 and widened during the 1920s. Immediately upstream on a small island are two strange carved statues. The oldest, known as Jonah with his large tongued fish and which originally came from the monastery of Bonshommes, a French Order established at Ashridge in Buckinghamshire, was put there in 1844 and the second arrived in 1953. They serve as crude flood markers: "When Jonah is covered—bad flood"; this is an understatement!

Until the late 18th century, Turvey was home to the Mordaunt family who used the moated Turvey Hall as the Dower House to their Northamptonshire estate. The family became established in the early 13th century under Eustace le Mordaunt and rapidly rose to prominence. John Mordaunt, knighted in 1503, was one of the Royal Commanders at Bosworth and Stoke, MP for Bedfordshire, Speaker of the House of Commons, High Steward of Cambridge University and as a benefactor founded a chantry at Turvey. His son, another John, Privy Councillor and Sheriff of Bedfordshire and Buckinghamshire, was raised to a baronetcy, Baron Mordaunt of Turvey, by Henry VIII in 1532. The title passed to yet another John, also a Privy Councillor under Queen Mary. There are three impressive alabaster memorials in the parish church of All Saints to these John Mordaunts, the second John lying above his two wives Ellen and Joan.

Amongst the more colourful members of the family was Charles Mordaunt, third Earl of Peterborough (1658-1735). Described as a "soldier, general, diplomat, scholar, wit and womaniser", he distinguished himself taking Barcelona during the Spanish Civil War. "The genius and energy of one man supplied the place of 40 battalions and Peterborough had the glory of taking, with a handful of men, one of the largest and strongest cities of Europe....Scarcely any General had ever done so much with means so small". He travelled extensively in Europe; "repose was insupportable to him". Repose finally came in Lisbon where he died and his body was returned to be buried at Turvey.

The Mordaunts were succeeded by the Higgins family. Charles Higgins (1806-1885), a devout man about whom it was said that he never cut his hair following a visit to Jordan, raised funds to build one of the first reformatory schools for young offenders in England, a few miles downstream at Carlton. In the parish churchyard is their large mausoleum inscribed "What man is he that liveth and shall not see death".

Harrold on the north bank, is linked with Carlton to the south by another long narrow ancient bridge first mentioned in 1279. Known as the Nun's Bridge, it was reputedly built by a prioress of the priory of canons and nuns founded by Sampson le Fort for the order of St Nicholas of Arronaria and later occupied by the prioress and nuns of the order of St Austin. Whilst nothing remains of the priory, which probably occupied the site where the former Harrold Hall stood for just over 300 years (1608-1961), the bridge with its five pointed and eight semicircular arches and the 19 arch footbridge, remain. In the mid 19th century, George Berkeley, the youngest son of the fifth Earl of Berkeley, took over the Harrold Hall as well as the Oakley Hunt Kennels. He was a colourful man who once publicly assaulted James Fraser, the publisher of Fraser's Magazine, and fought a duel with the journalist Dr. Maginn, who had respectively published and written an unfavourable review of his romance Berkeley Castle. On the Green are an eight sided Buttercross Market and an ancient unusual round stone built lock-up with a conical stone roof and studded oak door. It was used as a "cooling off" place for drunks and vagabonds.

Three almshouses (since vanished) were established in 1732 by a resident of Harrold, the Honourable Ann Jollife and her late-in-life husband, Dr. Richard Mead (1673-1754). After obtaining an MB in Padua, Richard became an expert in venomous snake bites. He was elected to the council of the Royal Society and became its vice president in 1717. Whilst in London he lived at a house in Great Ormond Street which was to become the Hospital for Sick Children. It was from here that he treated Sir Isaac Newton, Sir Robert Walpole and, as Royal Physician, George I and George II.

In contrast with Harrold church, which might have had some links with the early priory, but is now somewhat mutilated, Carlton church of St Mary the Virgin is one of the most complete two cell Saxon churches in the county. Amongst its rectors (1720-1771) was the diarist Benjamin Rogers. His diary, finally published in 1949, spanned 11 years from 1727 to 1738. On 25 March 1729 he records "ordered William Allen to be blooded for pleurisy". After William had been blooded twice comes the entry, "He died". He does not record what eventually happened to his son, who on 19 May 1733, "being about five years old fell backwards into the pottage pot just as it was taken boiling off the fire for dinner". Carlton has a very tenuous link with William Shakespeare; his future son-in-law was born there.

Chellington now immediately adjoins Carlton although in the past it would have been further to the north east around the isolated and redundant church of St Nicholas, standing on a bluff above the river. Probably either the plague or early enclosures resulted in this small village moving towards the larger village of Carlton.

In Odell, a short distance downstream, a castle was built by Walter de Wahull (or Wodhul, later Woodhall), who appears to have taken the village name (or vice versa). In 1633 this castle and manor were purchased by William Alston, whose family, which included Sir Thomas Alston who helped organise the County for Parliament against the King, lived there for the next 300 years. Odell has a less than tenuous link with Concord, New Hampshire. In 1634, Peter Bulkley, a puritan who had been rector since 1620, was deprived of his living because of his contempt for church ceremonies. In 1635 he emigrated to New England, where, a year later he founded the city of Concord. He remained there as pastor until his death in 1659.

The first of the series of meanders virtually surrounds Felmersham. For centuries the only river crossing was by ford; the bridge, built by subscription, was opened in 1818. Whilst it is a small village, Felmersham church of St Mary, standing on a small bluff, is a delightful rarity. Dating from about 1220, it was built as an outpost of the priors of Lenton in Nottinghamshire. To see such a perfect early English facade is rare; to see such a complete early 13th century ironstone church is even rarer. The tower contains only five bells. There used to be six, and according to a legend, one was thrown into the river due to "a quarrel between the monks of Felmersham and their beloved brethren at Odell".

Sharnbrook and Bletsoe lie on the outside of this meander. In terms of their ancestry, Sharnbrook is swamped by the much smaller village of Bletsoe. Earthworks mark the site of its castle, inhabited by the De Pateshull family until the middle of the 14th century after which the estate passed, through marriage, to the Beauchamp family. In 1421, the estate passed to Margaret, aged only 11 and heiress of the Beauchamps. She married twice, first to John St John, whose family was to inherit the castle and who were to become the Barons of Bletsoe and later the Earls of Bolingbrooke and secondly to John Beaufort, the first Duke of Somerset and grandson of John of Gaunt. By this second marriage she gave birth, supposedly in the castle, to a daughter, another Margaret, who was to become Countess of Richmond and Derby. In 1455 she married first, Edmond Tudor, Earl of Richmond and thus became the mother of the future King Henry VII. After Edmond's death in 1456, she married secondly, Henry Stafford the second Duke of Buckingham who was executed in 1483 at Salisbury and after which she married thirdly Lord Stanley, the first Earl of Derby.

Margaret was one of the first patrons of Caxton, she translated French devotional books, she founded Lady Margaret's Colleges in both Cambridge and Oxford, as well as Christ's College (1505) and St John's College (1508) in Cambridge. At her funeral in 1509, Bishop Fisher said, "Everyone who knew her loved her and everything she said or did became her".

Radwell, Milton Earnest, Pavenham and Stevington lie on the outside of the next meanders, whilst Oakley, like Felmersham, lies on the inside. Radwell and Milton Earnest are connected by a mid to late 18th century bridge also built by subscription. Pavenham and Oakley are connected by another ancient bridge, Stafford Bridge. Why it should be called Stafford is not known, but it is an ancient name; in about 1227 "Richard de Pabeham fell from a certain mare into the water of Stafford so that he died". A bridge certainly existed here in the mid 17th century and which eventually became the responsibility of Bedford County and the Duke of Bedford. It suffered considerable damage in 1820 from "ice drawn against it in great violence which forced out several stones in most of the arches" and five years later in a great flood. Now much rebuilt, two medieval segmental arches with chamfered ribs remain.

Pavenham was the home of three redoubtable Victorian gentlemen. One, Joseph Tucker, was a staunch teetotaller who established a reading room which provided tea and cocoa instead of beer. He made visitors sign the pledge, but they still got round him by bringing in their lunch time beer in teapots. Another was the vicar, John Linnell, who was accustomed to walking to and from Bedford. During these walks he carried the shopping bags of any women he overtook, such that he "came home festooned like a Christmas tree". He was not a man to be trifled with; when attacked by thieves one night he fought them to a standstill, and then made them kneel down and say the Lord's Prayer. The third was the son of Linnell's predecessor, Charles Wilson, an early missionary in Uganda, and who brought home four chiefs to present to Queen Victoria.

Whilst Pavenham had its teetotallers, the opposite might be said of Stevington. One of several curious carvings on the church's bench ends depicts two men drinking from a large single bowl. Perhaps this is a reference to a Church Ales Endowment when, just like Church Teas, beer was brewed and served for church purposes. "Drinking Bush Hill is the name of a hill towards the western boundary of the parish. The parishioners when beating the bounds on arrival at this place, used to dig a hole, jump in it and then drink to satiety". Perhaps more in keeping, however, is the ancient Holy Well close to the church, once frequented by many pilgrims in the Stevington Pilgrimage and which reputedly has never frozen nor dried up. Whilst, apart from a few hollows and depressions to the west of the church, there is no trace of the 13th century castle, there is a notable wayside cross. Is this the cross about which John Bunyan wrote of Christian coming "at a place somewhat ascending and upon that place stood a cross", and at which spot the "burden loosed from off his shoulders"?

(See colour section for larger photo)

Most of the parish of Oakley was acquired by the fourth Duke of Bedford in about 1737. Their hunting lodge was enlarged on a ducal scale to become Oakley House and it was from here that the Oakley Hunt was established by the fifth Duke of Bedford and by Samuel Whitbread.

Clapham, once a chapelry of Oakley, and now very much a suburb of Bedford immediately adjoins Oakley. Clapham Park, a late Victorian Gothic mansion was built for James Howard (1821-1889) an agriculturist and public health advocate, who took out patents for agricultural machines including the first iron wheeled plough and founded the Bedford Britannia Ironworks. He became mayor of Bedford in 1863 and MP for Bedford (1868) and Bedfordshire (1880).

Clapham Manor House was the home of Dr. Henry Hammond (1605-1660). He was chaplain to Charles I but was stripped of this post and confined in semi imprisonment by the Puritans. One of his fellow prisoners was Gilbert Sheldon who was to become Archbishop of Canterbury in 1663. Clapham church of St Thomas of Canterbury has a unique but ugly 26m high tower built by the inhabitants of Clapham in the 10th century and which tends to dominate the rest of the church. It was built partly as a guard tower for the nearby ford and, with its entrance high above ground level, partly as a refuge.

To the south of Oakley an early 19th century bridge leads to Bromham which in turn has its own early medieval bridge. In 1227 it was described as the Bridge of Bideham, in 1224 as the Bridge of Biddenham, in 1540 as the "Pontern de Bydenham" and in 1728 as Bromham Bridge. In 1281 it was broken by ice and a woman was carried away on an ice flow. Although she was seen passing under Bedford Bridge 6km away it is not known if she was saved. At the foot of the bridge there used to be a chantry to Our Lady and St Kateryn recorded in the early 16th century. Although it is long vanished, remains could still be seen in the late 19th century incorporated in the structure of the miller's house. In the late 18th century it was still only a foot and horse bridge, however in the early 19th century it was considerably reconstructed or even rebuilt with 26 semicircular arches and a width between the parapets of 5.5m.

On the edge of the river is Bromham Hall, built on the site of an earlier house and dating from the 16th century. One of its early owners was the Royalist Sir Lewis Dyve (1599-1669). It is said he escaped from a Parliamentary troop by swimming the river. His life long opponent was Sir Samuel Luke of Wood End in Cople. Not only did they professionally cross swords at Newport Pagnell, but they also had a very personal quarrel. After Sir Lewis had escaped, Sir Samuel completely sacked Bromham Hall. However, not long after when, Sir Lewes had driven the Parliamentary soldiers out of Bedford, he, Sir Lewis, went on to Cople where he took his revenge and "served" Sir Samuel's house "as his own had been by the sequestrators".

The two knights had contrasting lives. The Royalist, knighted in 1620, was arrested for conspiracy, fled to Holland, was imprisoned in the Tower, served in Ireland and finally took refuge in France. The Parliamentarian, knighted in 1642, was MP for Bedford, was present at Edgehill and Chalgrove Field and became scoutmaster-general of the Army of the Earl of Essex. He was a friend of the satirist Samuel Butler and is said to have been the model for Butler's *Sir Hudibras.*

In the parish church of St Owen there are memorials to the Dyve family one of which is an armoured knight lying between two ladies and which is purported to be Sir John Dyve (d1535). In all probability it was appropriated for him having been made 100 years earlier for one Thomas Wydville. There are also memorials to the Dyve's successors at Bromham Hall, the Trevor family. Thomas Trevor (1658-1730), raised to Baron Trevor of Bromham in 1712, was chief justice, judge and Lord Privy Seal, continuing his family's political careers.

As a whole, the Dyve family must have had a certain reputation for rough justice. In 1589 William Boteler who lived across the river at Biddenham refused to have a duel with Sir Lewis' father. He was ambushed and beaten up by Dyve's armed men. The Boteler family included another William who was Chairman of the County Parliamentary Committee during the Civil War. Perhaps the family were always Parliamentarians, which would, of course, explain the enmity with the Dyve family.

Just before the river makes its final turn towards Bedford is Kempston. Now a suburb of Bedford, it is an ancient village whose old British name was Caembes, fittingly meaning Tun by the Bend. At a large pagan cemetery spanning several generations, a number of large Saxon burial pots, known as "Buckelurnen" containing cremated remains and similar to others found in Cambridge and York, have been discovered. Some of the most interesting local finds, however, have been some fine and complex Anglo Saxon brooches, now in the Museum of Archaeology and Ethnology in Cambridge. There are two types; one has an oblong shaped head plate, triangular footplate with an arched bow between. The other, four of which have been found, are collectively known as the Kempston type. They are round with a separate backplate, ornamental front plate and a design of four stylised legs alternating with four faces.

Water lilies are a feature of the upper reaches of the River Great Ouse, particularly those at Kempston immortalised by Cowper.

> *It was the time when Ouse displayed*
> *His lilies newly blown:*
> *Their beauties I intent surveyed,*
> *and one I wished my own.*
> *With cane extended far I sought*
> *To steer it close to land,*
> *But still the prize, though nearly caught,*
> *Escaped my eager hand.*

However, here at Kempston on the outskirts of Bedford, a manor once held by Judith, William the Conqueror's niece, for an annual rent of one red sparrow hawk, the first of a series of significant character changes occurs. The river, which has gradually been becoming wider, becomes both wider and deeper. Suddenly, for the first time, downstream from Kempston Mill, motor cruisers appear on the river as it enters, coincidentally, the suburban and industrial outskirts of Bedford.

One such industry is Charles Wells' Eagle Brewery which borders the river close to Kempston. Charles Wells was born in Bedford in 1842. Leaving school at fourteen, he joined the frigate Devonshire for a maritime career, becoming Chief Officer in 1868. Reminiscent of the Olney curate John Newton, he had planned to marry his childhood sweetheart Josephine Grimbley, however his future father-in-law forbade the marriage because he did not want his daughter to marry a man who would be away for so much of his time. So, not to be thwarted, Charles embarked on his second career and founded Charles Wells Family Brewery in 1876. The family has carried on the business for four generations and the water is still drawn from an original well sunk almost 100 years ago.

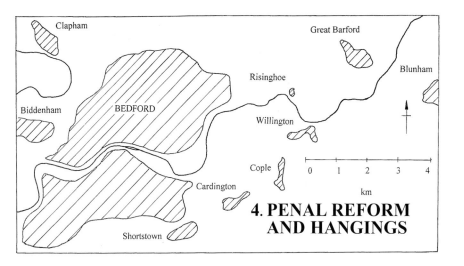

Clapham

Great Barford

Risinghoe

Blunham

Biddenham

BEDFORD

Willington

Shortstown

Cardington

Cople

0 1 2 3 4

km

4. PENAL REFORM
AND HANGINGS

The present effective upstream limit of navigation on the River Great Ouse is at the site of the old Kempston Mill, adjoining Bedford and some 142km from the mouth of the river at King's Lynn. The Danes, with their shallow draught longships, were amongst the first to navigate the River Great Ouse as far inland as Bedford. However, after Edward I's reign, the river was generally only navigable from King's Lynn to Huntingdon and occasionally to St Ives, above which navigation was restricted by numerous mills and associated weirs. Little was done to extend and improve navigation until the 17th century, when, in 1618, secretary of state Sir Clement Edmondes (1564? - 1622) was appointed by the Privy Council to investigate the true state of the lower river and its potential for navigation and trade. The extension of navigation to Bedford took place over several stages, the first significant works being carried out under the supervision of Arnold Spencer and Thomas Girton who had acquired the navigation rights in 1618 from John Gason. Arnold Spencer was a Bedfordshire man who lived close to the river at Cople, between Cardington and Willington; Thomas Girton was a Westminster vintner. Both were wealthy and shrewd business men and initially concentrated their efforts on improving navigation between Huntingdon and St Neots, building six sluices.

Shortly before his death, Thomas Girton transferred in 1625 his interests to Arnold Spencer, who in turn assigned all his rights to John Jackson of St Neots. Arnold Spencer, however, maintained his interest in navigation and began negotiations with the town of Bedford, to extend navigation, financing himself the necessary Act of Parliament.

All these plans and works, however, were interrupted by the Civil War and no progress was made until 1674 when Henry Ashley, a tanner of Eynesbury, obtained a lease for the navigation rights. Under his direction, navigation was once again improved in the lower reaches and extended to Great Barford. In 1687 he was appointed undertaker to extend navigation to Bedford, a task which he accomplished within two years and which included the building of the first sluices at Cardington, Castle Mills and Willington.

Throughout the 18th and the first half of the 19th century, commercial traffic, overall, steadily increased, reaching a plateau in about 1838. By 1841 the volume of river trade at Bedford was 13,600 tons and which produced an income from tolls of £7,139. However, despite this overall growth, by the end of the 18th century there were ominous signs of a decline. Traffic in coal at Bedford decreased by 28% between 1790 and 1821, a reduction attributed almost entirely to the growth in commercial traffic on the Grand Union Canal. This decline was accelerated by the growth of the railway network in the 1850s. Apart from some local commercial traffic, navigation upstream from Tempsford ceased in 1876. General navigation through to Bedford was not restored until the 1970s, some 20 years after the Great Ouse Restoration Society started its campaign for the improvement of the derelict 13km of river separating Bedford from the navigable River Great Ouse and the sea.

However, this would not all have been the case had some of the early 19th century proposals for a vast network of navigable waterways, aimed at increasing commercial river traffic, come to fruition.

In 1811, John Rennie, (1761 - 1821) an engineer with a great reputation for canal building, proposed a 24km canal with 25 locks and a feed reservoir to join the River Great Ouse near Kempston with the Grand Junction Canal (Grand Union Canal) at Fenny Stratford. Despite the support of prominent Bedfordshire families, John Russell, sixth Duke of Bedford, his son, the Marquess of Tavistock and the politician and brewer, Samuel Whitbread II, Rennie's liberal estimate of £180,807 proved too much for the proposition to be viable.

Both John Russell and Samuel Whitbread had had an interest in promoting river traffic, John continuing his family's long association with rivers; it was his great, great, great-grandfather Francis Russell, 4th Earl of Bedford who had subscribed to the 17th century draining of the fens. To ease both river and road traffic, they provided £2,000 each towards a new bridge. As the marquess had lost his money at the dogs, John Russell provided a further £500 as he wished his son's name to be included amongst the benefactors. The bridge, now called the Town Bridge, was opened in 1813. It was wider and with fewer piers than the old damaged stone bridge dating from the late 12th century, which it replaced. The first record of a bridge, with a chapel dedicated to St Thomas and whose chaplain was allowed to collect a toll for repairs to the bridge, was in 1179. It was reputedly repaired and rebuilt with stones from Bedford Castle, destroyed in 1224, and was greatly damaged in a great flood of 1671.

Under an Act of 1814, the Grand Union Canal near Wolverton was linked to the River Ouse at Newport Pagnell via a new 2.5km canal with seven locks. Because of the long, meandering, shallow and generally un-navigable nature of the Ouse between Newport Pagnell and Bedford, a proposal of 1817 suggested a new cut direct from Newport Pagnell to Kempston to bypass this stretch. This was to be extended to St Neots, thus bypassing another long, albeit navigable, stretch of the Ouse, and to Kimbolton on the River Kym.

Under the Hertford Union Canal Act of 1824, John Rennie's proposals were resurrected and combined with a plan to join the River Great Ouse, and hence the Grand Junction Canal, with Shefford and the River Ivel Navigation and on to Hitchin on the River Hiz and Hertford and the River Lee Navigation.

Although these and similar plans were considered throughout the 19th century, because of the sheer physical size and huge associated costs of the undertakings, none came to fruition. Indeed, the only scheme which had been constructed, the Newport Pagnell Canal, was closed in 1864 and ironically partially converted into a railway; the ultimate destroyer of commercial river and canal traffic.

However, with the considerable growth of leisure boating industry, some of these plans were to be revived nearly 200 years later. Whilst the River Ouse is linked to the Grand Union Canal near Gayton, it is a long and sometimes difficult route which runs from Denver, along a short tidal length of river, across the Fenland of the Middle Level to the River Nene at Peterborough, and then up the River Nene, to join the Northampton Arm of the Grand Union Canal at Cotton End, Northampton. It is about 150km from Denver to the main Grand Union Canal and there are 53 locks to navigate. Included in a scheme introduced in 1998 to promote interest in the Fenland waterways was a proposal once again to join the River Great Ouse at Bedford with the Grand Union Canal at Milton Keynes. The two towns are some 20km apart and there are essentially two possible routes. One, between Milton Keynes and Kempston would require extensive engineering works in Bedford where there are low bridges and narrow locks, but would revitalise the Bedford river front. The other longer route bypasses Bedford, thus avoiding the engineering works in the town, to join the River Ouse below Bedford near Newnham Priory. In either instance as many as 20 locks, and possibly a tunnel and boat lift will be required at an estimated cost of between £80m and £150m depending on the choice of route.

Should the scheme be realised, not only would it provide a relatively short and easy access to the Great Ouse but, for the more adventurous navigators, it would also afford a circular navigable route through all the East Anglian waterways. So whilst Kempston may remain as the present upstream limit of navigation on the River Great Ouse, it may also lie at or near the junction of a future Grand Union Canal to River Great Ouse link.

Whilst the Great Ouse throughout its length is a river of contrasting characters, Bedford provides more than its share, some of the most dramatic being associated with prisons, namely John Bunyan, John Howard and James Hanratty.

Arguably, John Bunyan was Bedford's greatest son. He was born in November 1628 at Elstow near Bedford, son of a tinsmith, Thomas Bunyan, and whose trade he was initially to follow. His mother died in 1644 and his father remarried. Provoked by this marriage, he enlisted in the Parliamentary forces serving at Newport Pagnell and it was during this time that he became deeply disturbed following the death of a comrade who had been standing in for him. Indeed throughout his early life he was haunted by religious fears and a sense of sin. However, after he had completed his two year service, he returned to the life of a tinsmith and resumed his boisterous life of bell-ringing, dancing, and playing "tip-cat", all punctuated with much cursing, swearing, lying and blaspheming, particularly during religious occasions. All this though was set to change when, following his marriage in his early twenties, his wife introduced him to devotional books and he finally gave up his bad habits for the Bible and church services.

The events which probably had the most impact on his life were the birth of his first daughter born blind in 1650, and, after giving him three more children, the death of his wife in c1656 in their new home in St Cuthbert's Street, Bedford. Although the church register of St Helen's Church in Elstow records his baptism in November 1628, a small plaque by an old backwater of the River Ouse records his baptism "circa 1650". It may well have been the birth of his blind daughter that prompted a renewed baptism. He joined religious societies and, although he was not licensed to do so, following the Restoration of the Monarchy when non-conformists were forbidden to preach, he began to preach. In November 1660, the year following his marriage to his second wife, Elizabeth, he was arrested and sentenced, in January 1661 for a "short" term of imprisonment in Bedford County Jail for continuing to preach without a licence. He refused to give an undertaking to stop public preaching and despite the efforts of his wife to secure an early release, he remained in the jail for the next 11 years. In 1672 he was released under Charles II's Declaration of Indulgence. However, some three years later he was back in prison again, possibly in the town jail near the river, but this time only for about two years. It was during this time that, it is believed, he wrote his Pilgrim's Progress. The complete work was published in 1678 and 100,000 copies were sold during his remaining life-time. It has become one of the best known books in the world and has been translated into more than 200 languages and dialects. Once out of prison he continued to write a further 40 books and to preach until he died of pneumonia in 1688.

Perhaps his sojourn close to the River Great Ouse inspired the truism:

...my great-grandfather was but a waterman,
looking one way and rowing another;
and I got most of my estate by the same occupation.

Bunyan's influence and his meeting house lasted well into the 18th century when it had over 100 members. For the early part of his life, John Howard lived next door. Born in about 1726, he was also a Dissenter and in the mid 1770s founded another meeting house, later known as the Howard Congregational Church. Surprisingly, for a Dissenter, he was made High Sheriff of Bedfordshire in 1773 and was recognised as an expert on the penal system. His interest started with Bedford County and City Jails.

Here he found appalling sanitary conditions. During the day men and women mixed together; during the night they had two very damp below ground dungeons. The only ventilation was provided by a "sail ventilator", built like a windmill, and installed in 1754. Fever, leading to death, was common. He also found that the jailers and turnkeys did not receive a salary. Instead they received a fee, 15/4d for the jailer and 4d for the turnkey, which had to be paid by every person who entered prison, whether guilty or eventually proved to be innocent, before they were discharged. He rapidly became an acknowledged expert in prisons and in 1774 he obtained Acts for the abolition of jailer's fees and for sanitary improvements. He went on to visit and inspect English, Scottish, Irish, French, Flemish, Dutch, German and Swiss prisons, bridewells and prison ships. In 1777 he published his *State of the Prisons* and 1780 an *Appendix to State of Prisons*. He continued to visit prisons throughout Europe. He died of camp fever in 1790 at Kherson whilst travelling with the Russian Army in the Ukraine. The following year the first General Prisons Act was passed and his legacy remains; the Howard League of Penal Reform. On his tomb in Russia was inscribed:

Whosoever thou art, thou standest at the grave of thy friend.

In direct contrast to these first prison reforms, the last man to be hanged in Britain was executed in Bedford prison. On the evening of August 21, 1961, Michael Gregsten, 36, a scientist, and his friend Valerie Storie, 22, were disturbed as they sat in their car near Maidenhead in Berkshire. They were forced to drive 96km to a lay-by on the A6 at Deadman's Hill near Bedford. Here Michael was shot and killed and Valerie raped, shot and left for dead. James Hanratty was charged with murder, charges of rape and attempted murder being held in reserve. He was tried in the red brick former Shire Hall on the bank of the river and was found guilty of murder, despite claiming he was 400km away at the time. Aged only 25, he was hung on 4 April 1962, since when his relatives have strongly maintained his innocence, claiming that the DNA tests linking him with the crime were unreliable.

(See colour section for larger photo)

In March 1999 the case was referred to the Court of Appeal by the Criminal Cases Review Commission and on 17 October 2001, Lord Wolf, the Lord Chief Justice concluded that "...it would be desirable for James Hanratty to be exhumed in the interests of justice". After 40 years, the speculation which has surrounded this case may be concluded.

If John Bunyan was Bedford's most famous "natural" son, then Glen Miller must have a justified claim to be the town's most famous adopted son. Born on 1 March 1904 in Clorinda, Iowa, he developed an early interest in music and despite his family's wishes started trombone lessons in 1916. He did eventually enter University, but left in 1926 to join Ben Pollack's band as a trombone player. Between 1929 and 1931 he played with such famous jazz and big band swing musicians as Benny Goodman, Red Nichols and the Dorsey Brothers. His first orchestra which he set up in 1937 only lasted a few months because of lack of funds. He tried again in 1938 and by 1939 achieved success with the two hits *Moonlight Serenade* and *Sunrise Serenade*. After a string of further hits, including *Pennsylvania 6-5000*, a tribute to the old Pennsylvania Hotel in Manhattan, scene of some of his greatest successes, *Chattanooga Choo Choo, A String of Pearls* and *American Patrol*, in September 1942, he was drafted into the American Army with the rank of Captain.

Although his orchestra had to break up, he set up his famous Army Airforce Band, composed entirely of professional musicians serving with the American forces. Based at Bedford, he played regularly for the BBC and flew frequently to war-torn Europe to give concerts. On one such trip, on 15 December 1944, he set off with a fellow American officer for Paris, a trip from which, as Major Glen Miller, he was destined never to return, his plane being lost over the English Channel. The *St Louis Blues March* recorded in July 1944 is a fitting epitaph for a man whose records still sell in thousands all over the world.

A little downstream from Bedford, the theme of disastrous air travel, albeit from a somewhat earlier age, is continued. Although not strictly on the River Great Ouse, a little to the south across a bridge designed by John Smeaton, a contemporary of John Rennie, and like him, an expert on canals and arched bridges, the two vast, stark hangers which once housed the airships R100 and R101 are clearly visible, silhouetted against the sky at Cardington. In 1908 Oswald Short an aeronautical engineer, who in 1898 had founded a showman-aeronaut business with his brother Eustace, founded with his second brother Horace, the company Short Brothers. In 1917, however, the Government took over their works and it was here that the airships R100 and R101 were built.

The "R" stood for Rigid. Essentially there were three designs of airships, non-rigid, semi-rigid and rigid. The non-rigid type, sometimes known as a "blimp", was simply a long gas balloon with the engine/passenger car suspended below it. The semi-rigid type in which a long rigid keel supported the cars was largely developed by the Italians. The rigid airships, developed by the Germans and British, contained their gas bags in a lattice of light alloy metals. Whilst the British R34, built in 1919 made the first ever double crossing of the Atlantic, British craft, unlike the German *Zeppelins*, did not generally take part in a regular passenger service.

The R101 was the largest and most luxurious to be built at Cardington, however, during her maiden voyage to India on 5 October 1930, she crashed in flames at Beauvais in France with the loss of 49 lives. In St Mary's Church the airship's scorched ensign hangs above a memorial plaque; the victim's tomb is in the churchyard across the street. Amongst the victims was Lord Thomson of Cardington, Minister of Air. The disaster discouraged, for the time being, further building in Britain and the R100, which had flown to Canada and back, was dismantled for scrap.

Ultimately the Short brothers became responsible for the design of flying boats and the construction of the Empire Flying Boats of Imperial Airways and for Sunderlands and Stirlings for the RAF. Close to the hangers, a little to the west of Cardington, they built the garden village of Shortstown for their labourers.

(See colour section for larger photo)

Howard's House, opposite the north east corner of the graveyard was the last home of John Howard; he left it to his cousin Samuel Whitbread, founder of the Whitbread Brewery, who had been born in Cardington in 1720. Both men did much to improve the village of Cardington. They strove that "which shall most benefit and adorn it". Not only was John Howard a friend of Samuel Whitbread , but so was Josiah Wedgwood, who aged nine was a "thrower" at Burslem, Staffordshire and 20 years later opened his own pottery works also at Burslem with the help of his brother Thomas. In particular he improved not only ordinary ware, Egyptian ware and marbled ware but also basaltic ware. In the Whitbread Chapel in St Mary's Church there is a Wedgwood Font, one of only three other known examples, the two others being in a private collection in America, and the other in Essende in Hertfordshire.

The Whitbread Chapel in St Mary's Church, which stands on the site of an earlier Anglo Saxon church, commemorates Samuel Whitbread I (1720-1796) and Samuel Whitbread II (1764-1815). The latter, a radical politician, became the Whig MP for Bedford in 1790. He became a close friend of Charles Fox, a leader of the opposition to William Pitt's government and champion to Caroline, Princess of Wales. Following his surprising suicide on 6 July 1815, his obituary in the *Northampton Mercury* describes a man who was "...the earnest and indefatigable friend of the oppressed...wearied out by no difficulties and exhausted by no fatigues...In his friendships no man was more ready to sacrifice life, ease and comfort than himself." In the village, houses bear the letters "SW", a testament to their efforts.

To the north of Cardington, as the river leaves Bedford, is the site of the Augustinian Newnham Priory. Now only a few over-grown earthworks remain of what was one of the oldest foundations in the county of Bedfordshire. It was founded in c1166 after the succession of Henry II, by Roisia de Beauchamp and her son Simon as a priory for Augustinian canons. It is said that it was founded here because, until 1164, St Paul's Church in

Bedford was served by a college of Black canons who had their town house. In that year there was a quarrel between town and church; one of the townsfolk was killed. Not only that, but one of the canons, Philip de Broc was implicated. It was at a time when a controversy about criminal jurisdiction by the State above the Clergy was at its height. Feeling ran high in the town and Philip and the canons retreated to Newnham where Roisia built them their priory, from whence they continued to serve St Paul's.

Its early materialistic period was inextricably linked to Bedford Castle. Whilst it had a good reputation, it suffered during King John's reign when much was pulled down in order to strengthen Bedford Castle, which consequently became one of the most formidable castles of the time. Never the less during the great siege of Bedford Castle in June 1224, and which lasted about seven and a half weeks, it was destroyed. Those that surrendered, about 80, were sentenced to death by the young King Henry and hung. Many of the stones of the former castle were returned to the priory. Consequent upon the Dissolution of the Monasteries, the priory was surrendered in c1540. The old site has recently been further considerably altered by the Cambridge to Bedford railway line (1862-1966) which passed straight through the centre.

The castle's stones were destined to be moved again to build, amongst other things, the house and outbuildings of the man who had been instrumental in its surrender, Sir John Gostwick. In the early 16th century, Sir John was an important Bedfordshire landowner who lived at Willington and who served Cardinal Wolsey and assisted Henry VIII in the destruction of the Bedfordshire monasteries. Of his Tudor mansion there are, following a fire, a few remains built into the present manor house. What do remain are an early 16th century dovecote, with stepped gables, a two tiered roof and nesting holes for around 1,500 doves, and a two floored stable, also with stepped gables. These buildings are close to the church of St Lawrence, which may have also been built or rebuilt by Sir John in the late perpendicular style and which houses fine alabaster monuments to the family. His coat of arms portrays on the chief, three horses heads instead of proper representation of his family. Instead they allude to his office of Master of the Horse to Henry VIII.

Not only did the Cambridge to Bedford railway line pass through Newnham Priory, but it also passed through earthworks, ramparts and moats at Willington. Close to the river these are the remains of Danish docks which once had moorings for up to 30 ships and accommodation for about 2,500 men. The Danish Great Army or "Host" had arrived and settled in East Anglia in 865, led by Ivar the Boneless and Halfdan, sons of a Viking, Ragnar Lothbrok, famous in Scandinavian legends. Under a treaty between King Alfred and the Danish King Guthrum in c890, England was divided into the Mercia to the west and the Danelaw to the east. Its boundary ran from the River Thames, up the River Lea to Hertford, round Hertford north in a straight line to the River Ouse just east of Bedford and thence along the River Ouse upstream to Fenny Stratford. Willington, just in the Danelaw, lay on this boundary and as such would have been a very important frontier outpost. It, and perhaps nearby Risinghoe Castle on the opposite bank, were probably associated with the Dane's final advance from Huntingdon to Bedford.

In c918 jarl Thurcytel, almost all the other Scandinavian barons and other chief men at Bedford submitted to King Edward at Buckingham, and the following year the King moved his army to Bedford Castle. In c921 the Danes advanced again from Huntingdon towards Bedford, building a new fortress on the way at Tempsford. They were repulsed by King Edward's army and retreated to Tempsford where they were attacked again. The fortress was seized, the Danish King and many Danish noblemen were killed, and the remainder of the Danish army were taken prisoner. It was the beginning of the end for that phase of Danish aggression in East Anglia, King Edward's final victory being at Maldon later that year.

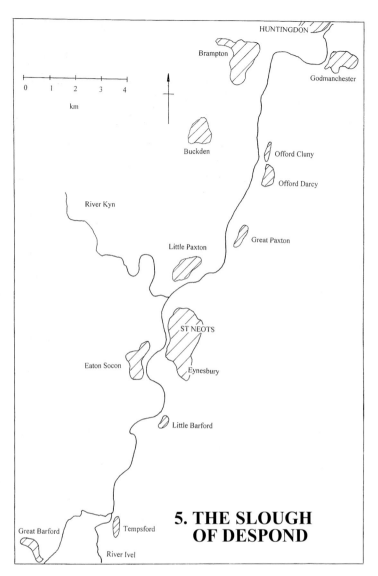

HUNTINGDON

Brampton

Godmanchester

0　1　2　3　4
km

Buckden

Offord Cluny

Offord Darcy

River Kyn

Great Paxton

Little Paxton

ST NEOTS

Eaton Socon

Eynesbury

Little Barford

**5. THE SLOUGH
OF DESPOND**

Great Barford

Tempsford

River Ivel

Before reaching Tempsford, the river flows under Great Barford bridge, arguably the most elegant bridge on the Great Ouse. In his will of 1429, Sir Gerard Braybrooke, distantly related to Henry de Braybroc, Sheriff of Bedfordshire in the early 13th century, expressed a wish that a bridge, "be performed and finished" at Great Barford for which purpose he had left some money. In 1446 the Burgesses of Bedford appealed, ironically as later events would prove, for rent to complete the works. Completed in the mid 15th century, it was a substantial stone bridge with 17 irregular arches and upstream cut waters. Although restored and widened on the upstream side, much of the original lower stone work remains.

It was to have a significant impact on Bedford itself and upon the surrounding countryside. It was a stronger, wider and altogether better bridge than the late 12th century narrow stone bridge in Bedford. Consequently it took away much traffic and business from Bedford, so much so that the Burgesses, having first supported the bridge, now complained that it caused trade to bypass their town. It was mainly for this reason that townspeople were successful in reducing a tax due to the crown, the fee-farm rent, by a half. Trade soon became established near the substantial road bridge and river crossing, and until 1689, it was the head of navigation, with many shops, wharves, warehouses and pubs and inns for the lightermen.

If Tempsford was the site of the Dane's fortress which was destroyed by Edward I, then its actual site is almost certainly the ancient, moated, overgrown, but rather small Gannock's Castle, built not next to the River Great Ouse but on the east bank of the River Ivel, shortly upstream from their junction. It would have been a strategic site and perhaps deceptive as it was not built directly on the principle river. Not only were the Danes turned back here by Edward I, but they were to return in 1009, this time from the River Thames, through Oxfordshire and Buckinghamshire to the River Great Ouse, then downstream along the river through Bedford and past the Willington Docks as far as Tempsford. Whatever course of action was recommended to King Ethelred the Unready, it was never followed and by the following year the Danes had overrun much of England including Buckinghamshire, Bedfordshire and half of Huntingdonshire. They continued to rule until Edward the Confessor was acclaimed King in 1042. This, however, would not be the last time the Danes inhabited Tempsford.

41

The River Ivel, is the third significant tributary to join the River Great Ouse.

"Another thing is scarce to be equallid in the whole of Britain; Namely, that tho' the Ouse, by a long and winding course, cuts through the county and by its long reachings, so as to make above seventy miles between Oulney and St Neots, tho' not above twenty by land, yet in all that course it receives but one river into it, namely the little River Ivel, which falls into the Ouse a little above Tempsford."　　　　　　　　　　　　　D. Defoe.

It became a navigable waterway under the River Ivel Navigation Act of May 1757 and remained so until 1876 when it was finally closed to commercial craft. It is said, however, that it was used to carry traffic to Ely some 400 years earlier.

On 22 February 1322, the eve of the feast of St Eormenilda, just as the Monks were returning from Ely Cathedral to their dormitory, the old Norman central tower built by Abbot Simeon c1084, fell, "with such a shock and so great a tumult that it was thought an earthquake had taken place". No one was killed and none of the shrines of the three Abbesses, Saints Etheldreda, Sexburga, and Withburga were damaged. Alan of Walsingham was appointed to redesign and rebuild the central tower. It was to be crowned by an octagonal lantern tower, each corner of which was to be built of wood, two huge oak tree trunks being placed one on top of the other, the whole then clad with lead. It was completed in c1341.

There is an account that Alan had great difficulty in finding straight oak tree trunks 19m long, but when he did, he transported them by "land and sea to Ely". There is another theory that he found them in extensive woodlands near Chicksands Gilbertine priory and transported them via the Rivers Ivel and Great Ouse to Ely. Both accounts can be reconciled, bearing in mind that at the time the causeways to Ely were in bad condition and the Isle was in effect surrounded by sea. If the trunks were indeed transported in this manner, it presupposes that by the early 14th century at the very latest, the River Great Ouse flowed without a break towards Ely. The priory had been founded in 1154, by Rose de Beauchamp of Bedford Castle, for nuns. At one time 120 nuns had 55 brothers for company!

If Tempsford had this early connection with civil engineering and building, it certainly has a modern connection recognised throughout the world. Tempsford Hall, built in Elizabethan style in 1898 on the site of an earlier house, is the headquarters of the Kier Group. The former hall was the home of Sir Gillies Payne who had made his fortune from sugar plantations in the West Indies in the mid 18th century. In 1824, the Payne family sold the hall to William Stuart, a grandson of the Earl of Bute and who rebuilt much of it in 1874. Twenty four years later the entire house was destroyed by fire. After rebuilding in 1902, again by the Stuart family, the house was occupied by the family and later various leaseholds until 1965 when it was bought by the Kier Group, founded by the Danish civil engineer Olaf Kier. The Danes had returned! In the space of 35 years, the Group had grown into a major international construction group employing over 6,500 people worldwide, with a turnover approaching £1bn.

The next stretch between Great Barford and St Neots is arguably the least attractive of the upper river, although it is not as bad as described in a survey of 1618: "generally foul and overgrown with weeds". That survey, however, gives credence to the view expressed by some that a marshy area around the ford at Tempsford, which during the winter, readily turned into a swamp, was in fact John Bunyan's "Slough of Despond" lying between the "City of Destruction", (Bedford) and the "Hill of Difficulty". This ancient ford was the principle river crossing for the Great North Road until at the latest 1776. Indeed an interpretation of Tempsford is Ford on the Road to the Thames, i.e. to London. Tempsford Staunch, built in 1674, was kept open for as long as possible to ensure a shallow river crossing. Only when road traffic was light was it closed so that navigation could proceed. The first bridge was built in c1813 and the staunch removed in the 1970s.

Of the many authors and poets who have lived near the river, one was born in a small thatched cottage at Little Barford in 1674. Although he trained initially in the legal profession, becoming a barrister in Middle Temple, Nicholas Rowe abandoned that career in 1692 to become a playwright, more successful with his tragedies than his comedies. In 1715, three years before his death, he was appointed Poet Laureate. His collected works, which make no reference to the River Great Ouse, were published posthumously in 1727.

Opposite Rowe's Cottages, a footpath leads to an old ferry crossing and the redundant church of St Dennis, around which, judging from the large area of hummocky ground, there was once a sizeable riverside village. The ferry crossing was somewhat of an accident blackspot. In December 1267, four people were drowned when attempting to cross with a load of flour, and a few years later the ferryman himself was drowned.

In direct contrast, one of the biggest single industrial sites on the river is the National Power Little Barford power station. It was first built in 1945/7 in a massive concrete cubic style reminiscent of London's old Battersea Power Station. For years its massive cooling towers dominated the landscape for miles around.

If the river flows out of Bedfordshire on an industrial note, it flows into the former county of Huntingdonshire, now a district of Cambridgeshire, on an urban note as it passes through a "conurbation" collectively called St Neots but actually made up of Eaton Socon with its castle and Eaton Ford to the west and Eynesbury and St Neots with its priory to the east.

(See colour section for larger photo)

At Eaton Socon, in Bedfordshire until the 1960s, a powerful barony became established in a castle built by Eudo Dapifer, a Steward to the Royal Household and which later became one of the Beauchamp strongholds. Excavations have revealed about 40 late Saxon burials and evidence of a church and other buildings suggesting that the castle had been built over an earlier pre-Norman settlement, strategically positioned on the river bank and no doubt controlling a strategic river crossing. Indeed, the name Eaton Socon, "the Hamlet on the river" and "a District with a right of jurisdiction", hence "the village by the Ouse subject to a jurisdiction other than that of the surrounding district" imply a village of some early prominence. All that remains now of that former Bedfordshire stronghold is a large moated mound with a smaller one superimposed, and two moated baileys.

Across the river and the old county boundary is Eynesbury, the "mother" parish of St Neots, from which it is separated by the Hen Brook. If Eaton Socon was a Bedfordshire garrison manor, Eynesbury was a Huntingdonshire religious manor from which St Neots was to grow. In 974 Earl Leofric, with the agreement of Ely, founded the Benedictine priory of St Neot. St Neot was a Cornish soldier who turned to become a revered monk and a friend and a tutor and advisor to King Ælfred. According to legend he was a very small man, less than one half a metre tall, and a tale is told that when he was attempting to admit a visitor, the door latch slid down the door of its own accord to his reach. He died in c877 and was buried at St Neot in Cornwall. A hundred years later Leofric, anxious to obtain a relic, had his remains removed, legally or illegally, to his Benedictine priory at Eynesbury.

The small priory has had a chequered history. It was destroyed during the Danish wars, only to be refounded in the late 11th century by Richard and Aroysia de Clare who wanted it removed from the control of Ely to the Abbey of Bec in Normandy. When Richard died, Aroysia gave it all over to the monks in 1113 in memory of her late husband. The monks formed their own lands and tenants into a community and so St Neots was founded. The priory suffered some decline during the Hundred Years War, since it was considered to be "foreign". It became independent of the Abbey of Bec in 1412; all but two of the monks returned to France. It grew again only to be abandoned after the Dissolution of the Monasteries in the mid 16th century when 11 monks were in residence. Its stones were used for the stone bridge built later that century and the gatehouse remained until 1814.

The site was generally unoccupied until 1584 when the Crown leased to Edward Catley, a mill, brewhouse and mill house by the priory gatehouse for 50 years at a rent of £4/year and so the Priory Brewery was born. In 1764 William Fowler was the brewer who built over all the remains of the priory. Later John Day took over the brewery which continued in operation until its closure in 1919.

St Neots, like Bedford, had many other breweries which became established towards the end of the 18th century. One such was that started by William Foster who, with Samuel Einey, owned the Bull Inn. It was purchased in 1831 by James Paine and brewing continued there until the Paine family disposed of the title in 1982. Brewing continued under the title of James Paine Brewery Ltd until 1987, when brewing eventually ceased at St Neots and the company was taken over by Tollemache and Cobbold of Ipswich.

If Eynesbury has an original claim to a midget, it also has a claim to a giant. James Toller, the Eynesbury Giant, was born in 1798, and grew to a height of 2.6m. In spite, or perhaps because, of his height, he had a delicate health and died aged 20. It is said that he is buried, instead of in the graveyard, under the font of the parish church of St Mary, in order to frustrate grave robbers and body snatchers.

At Little Paxton, a former corn mill was converted into a paper mill by Henry and Sealy Fourdrinier. The brothers were inventors and in 1807 they invented a continuous paper making machine at a cost of £60,000. Unfortunately they did not take out the appropriate patents and the small mill was overtaken by their competitors. Whilst they became bankrupt, they received a parliamentary grant in 1840 for losses sustained. The mill, converted to steam power in 1851, was taken over by Matthew Towgood who kept it open until 1880 when it was closed for eight years until being taken over by a consortium, the St Neots Paper Mill Co.

On the opposite bank of the river is Great Paxton, now a quarter the size of Little Paxton. The Saxon minster church of Holy Trinity is claimed to be unique in England. Of the original church, built c1020, both the nave arcades and a crossing have survived the rebuilding of the 13th and 15th century, the former of resulting in an elevated chancel, some 3m above the nave. Thankfully full "Victorian Restoration" in 1880 was sympathetically carried out.

Offord Cluny marks another site connected with a French abbey. Cluny Abbey in Burgundy owned the manor from pre Doomsday up to the early 15th century. Almost opposite is the Anglia Water intake and pumping station for the nearby Grafham Water reservoir. This is amongst the largest man-made reservoirs in England. Excavated between 1962 and 1965 under the Great Ouse Water Act 1961, it was opened by the Duke of Edinburgh on 6 July 1966. Costing some £12 million, it covers some 810ha, with a shore line extending nearly 16km, and has a storage capacity of 60 million cubic metres. Despite vigorous protests, seven farms and 20 houses disappeared below the water surface. It derives 98.9% of its water from the River Great Ouse, and, depending on conditions, 3/4 of the river flow can be abstracted. Whilst it directly supplies a population some 562,000, it is linked with

Rutland Water and Pitsford reservoir and their combined output supplies about 1.5 million people.

A road leads west from Offord Cluny lock and mill to Buckden, which although it is 2km from the river deserves a special mention. Since before Domesday, the Manor of Buckden (Bugden), had been held by the Diocese of Lincoln, the largest diocese in medieval England. When travelling round their vast estate, the Bishops needed somewhere to stay. Although there was probably a residence for them by 1066, there are records of the existence of a house, (palace), and court by the middle of the 12th century. The house was rebuilt and a Great Hall added in the early to mid 13th century. In 1291 it was rebuilt again following a fire, and a redbrick tower had been added by 1480. This 15th century brickwork is one of the finest examples in the county. By the end of the 16th century, however, the large palace was a ruin, which was eventually repaired, but on a much smaller scale, in 1660 for Bishop Sanderson. During its lifetime many Bishops used this palace as their principal residence and never even visited their cathedral in Lincoln. The last time the palace was occupied by a Bishop was in 1838. It was sold by the diocese in 1870 and again in 1957 to the Catholic Church and is used by the Order of Claretian Missionaries. Those who stayed at the palace include Henry III, Edward I, Catherine of Aragon, Henry VIII, Catherine Howard and the Prince Regent.

Perhaps Henry III liked the area because he is supposed to have stayed in a royal residence at Brampton; Henry I, Stephen, Henry II and King John likewise. The residence, dating from before the Norman conquest, was supposedly destroyed by floods in 1348. The present red brick Manor House, built in 1875 and which became the Huntingdonshire police headquarters for a short time before becoming a Cheshire Home, is said to stand on the site of the old residence. As this site stands well above the flood plain, one or other of these suppositions seems incorrect.

Around a small green is a chapel, a number of small cottages marked with the letters "OBS" and Lady Sparrows School. Widowed in 1805, Lady Olivia Bernard Sparrow inherited the Bernard estate and lived at Brampton Park in a rebuilt mid 17th century house which stood on the site of 12th and 13th century cottages. She was much concerned with the welfare of her tenants, both temporally and spiritually, rebuilding their houses, donating a village school and founding a small hospital for the elderly in a house with an eight sided chimney. In 1889 she founded the Institution for the Care of Stammerers which was based in the Park until 1907 when the house was burnt down. Whilst a smaller house was built on the site, most of the Park was given over to the RAF to become the combined forces Logistics Command Headquarters.

Dating from the early 17th century, the Black Bull Pub in Brampton is said to have been Goody Stankes Ale House, where the beer, according to Samuel Pepys, "had just a touch of wormwood which delighted his palate".

Although born in London in 1633, the diarist Samuel Pepys lived for a while with his parents, who are buried in the parish church of St Mary the Virgin, in a house dating from the mid 16th century between Brampton and Huntingdon. He attended the Free School in Huntingdon, where some 34 years earlier Oliver Cromwell had also received his elementary education. Whilst he lived for most of his life in London, he retained a great interest in Huntingdonshire and was Secretary to his father's first cousin Edward Montagu, Earl of Sandwich at Hinchingbrooke House. It is said that he hid a pot of silver coins in his parents' garden fearing either the plague or a Dutch invasion; an iron pot containing silver coins was found there c1842.

Before reaching Godmanchester, the River Great Ouse and a tributary, the Alconbury Brook, encompass the "island" of Port Holme Meadow. First mentioned in 1205 as (?) the great meadow of Brampton, it is a Site of Special Scientific Interest, comprising some 104ha, and is claimed to be the largest tree-less meadow in England, where Marsh Dandelion, Brown Sedge, Great Burnett, Cowslips and Snakes Head Fritillary grow. The meadow was not always as peaceful as it appears now; variously it has been the venue for cock fighting, the site of the first Huntingdon racecourse, a first world war training airfield and the setting for a flying circus. Ancient footpaths cross the meadow between Brampton, Godmanchester and Huntingdon.

Godmanchester, known locally as "Gumster" (Gumecestre in 13th century) is arguably the oldest town in Huntingdonshire. From Bronze Age origins, it grew into an important Roman posting station on the major road junction of Ermine Street (London to York), the via Devana (from Cambridge), and a military road connecting Sandy with a fort at Godmanchester. Inns, temples, a guest house for Imperial visitors, a bathhouse, a bridge, and town walls were built during the 2nd and 3rd centuries.

Under a charter of 1212, King John gave the town a rare form of self government in return for an annual payment of £120. For nearly 400 years residents were free men, entitled to a degree of self government. They were not, however, allowed to sell or give away land which, according to an unusual custom, passed to the youngest son of the first wife. Sons and daughters that continued to live in the town became freemen and women at the age of 21 and were entitled to income from the common lands.

Two features of Godmanchester are the Chinese Bridge and a "Tide" clock. The "Chinese" or "Willow Pattern" bridge was built across a backwater in 1827 and has been rebuilt twice. The "Tide" clock is on the south side of the chancel of the church of St Mary. It takes the form of a very rare Mass dial in the shape of a wheel with trefoiled arches between eight spokes, each representing a period of one and a half hours starting, according to Saxon reckoning, at 6 am.

St Mary's Church, whose vicar was murdered by the townspeople in the 14th century, stands at the centre of several Roman cemeteries. Its graveyard contains an old burial ground for Nonconformists; their tombstones are laid at right angles to the those of the Church of England faith. One such tombstone is a replica memorial to Mary Anne Weems. Following a courtship and a compulsory marriage, her husband, Thomas, lured her away to Wendy, near Saffron Waldon, where he murdered her. Unfortunately for him, he was seen by a woman tending a sick cow. She stopped a passing coach which just happened to be carrying a JP. Thomas was caught, taken to Royston, and tried in Cambridge where he was executed in 1819.

Ere crime you perpetrate, survey this stone
Learn hence the God of Justice sleeps not on his throne
But marks the sinner with unerring eye
The suffering victim hears and makes the guilty die.

Control of the River Great Ouse has long been an issue in Godmanchester. In the 13th century sluices were in place at Hartford, Houghton, and Hemingford Grey mills. During the 15th century these resulted in Godmanchester suffering from continual flooding, so much so that in 1524 the right to control the sluices was given to the Borough. It was through the exercise of these rights that the need for public control of navigation and related matters first became a real issue. In 1893, a wealthy stockbroker, Leonard Simpson, bought the navigation rights on the river for £6,170 and started to restore the now derelict navigation to Bedford at a cost of up to £21,000. He suffered a number of set backs not least of which followed a severe flood in 1894. Godmanchester Corporation had exercised its ancient rights to open the sluice gates to relieve the town of flood waters. In so doing two of the gates were damaged. Believing that the gates belonged to him, Leonard Simpson took action against the Corporation and in a case which eventually went to the House of Lords in 1897, he was defeated. Angry at the decision, he decided to close navigation by padlocking 'his' gates and sinking barges in front of them. Unfortunately for him, Huntingdonshire County Council did not share that view and after a series of suits at The Court of Chancery, the Court of Appeal and the House of Lords, it was ruled that the public were entitled to pass through his locks, tolls could only be levied on commercial vessels and, perhaps surprisingly, he did have the right to close the locks. His attempts to restore the navigation had proved to be disastrously expensive and unprofitable.

A raised causeway leads to Huntingdon and a tablet on a bridge over a backwater commemorates an event which occasioned the first raising of the road.

Robertus Cooke ex aquis emersus hoc viatoribus sacrum. D.D. 1637.

Robert Cooke was a Master of the Hospital of St John in Huntingdon who was nearly drowned whilst trying to cross between Godmanchester and Huntingdon during a flood. The main stream of the Great Ouse, was crossed by a bridge dating from 1332. Building apparently started from each bank but unfortunately did not meet exactly; there is a slight bend near the central pier! There is no trace of the bridge chapel dedicated to St Thomas of Canterbury which, by 1572, had been converted into two shops. Whilst this ancient bridge is still in use today, it is completely dominated, both visually and noisily, by a massive concrete bridge carrying the A14, one of the busiest trunk roads in the country, over and around Huntingdon.

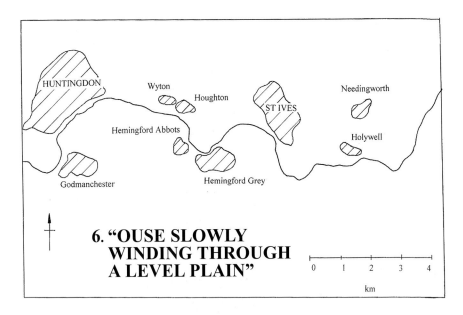

6. "OUSE SLOWLY WINDING THROUGH A LEVEL PLAIN"

Huntingdon has gone through several cycles of prosperity and poverty. It became a Danish trading centre with a fortress but which was abandoned in favour of Tempsford in 921. Edward the Elder rebuilt the fortress, an Anglo Saxon mint was established in 955 and a Norman Castle built on the site of the old fortress in 1098. It suffered badly during King Stephen's reign, only to recover and prosper during the late 13th and early 14th centuries. It developed a thriving religious community and at one time there were a Jewry, three Hospitals, a nunnery nearby at Hinchingbrooke, 16 churches, a priory of Austin canons, and a house of Austin friars.

It was, perhaps somewhat ironically, in the prior house of this latter house, dating from 1258, that Huntingdon's most famous, or some might say infamous, son Oliver Cromwell was born in 1599. He was christened in All Saints Church which stands on the site of an early Minster and he received his early schooling in the Huntingdon Free School, housed in the only remaining part of the Infirmary of the Hospital of St John the Baptist, founded in 1160 by David, Earl of Huntingdon. He continued to live in Huntingdon, becoming its MP in 1628 and JP in 1630, until 1631, when, now as a strict Puritan, he moved on to St Ives, Ely and London. Although no longer living in the town, he used the Falcon Inn for a time as his headquarters during the Civil War and he recruited many of his troops from the town and the county.

Oliver

Leaving Huntingdon, the river flows past Hartford Meadows, the site of the short lived Hospital of St Giles without Huntingdon, founded in the thirteenth century but disappeared by the time of the Black Death, to Hartford. One of the most attractive stretches of the river lies between Hartford and Holywell. According to William Cowper, who had lived in Huntingdon between 1765 and 1767:

> *Here Ouse,*
> *slowly winding through a level plain*
> *of spacious meads*
> *with cattle sprinkled o'er,*
> *conducts the eye along*
> *its sinuous course,*
> *Delighted.*

Hartford, originally Herford, or in the Doomsday Book, Hereford, has nothing to do with "harts" or "stags" from the nearby and long since vanished Royal Forest of Sapley. Its name means the "Ford of the Invading Army". Who were the invaders? Whilst most likely they were the Romans during their conquest of Britain, they could have been the Danes. The road to this old ford passes Hartford's church of All Saints, dating from the late 12th century charmingly poised on the river bank and a favourite haunt of William Cowper; "The church there is very prettily situated upon a rising ground, so close to the river that it washes the wall of the churchyard".

Another question is asked of Hartford. Who lost, or hid, 1,108 French and English coins, many of which were silver, in mint or near mint condition and dating between 1450 and 1503? Known as the Hartford Hoard, they were found in 1964 in an urn close to the old road from the ford and between two inns, the King of the Belgians and the Barley Mow, declared to be Treasure Trove and are now in the British Museum.

Between Hartford and St Ives, a number of locks, sluices, weirs and backwaters are evidence of the attempted dominance of the river by the mill owners of the mid-17th century and the consequent conflict with those seeking to navigate the river and those who were trying to prevent flooding. First, the mill owners, who believed they had first claim to the water, built the weirs to provide a sufficient head of water to turn the mill wheels. However, in so doing they not only prevented navigation but also restricted flood flows. As a part of the early stage in opening through navigation to Bedford, Arnold Spencer and Thomas Girton, built sluices, at Houghton and Hemingford Grey in 1630 and 1618 respectively and a staunch at St Ives.

So what is or was a "sluice" and a "staunch"? Sluices were in fact straightforward pound locks with two sets of gates which "open & shutt alternately as the boates come in & go out". They cost considerably more than staunches; typically £250 as opposed to £100. Staunches were simple barriers with one gate built across a river to control upstream water levels. When the barrier was open, which was the general tendency, upstream fords were shallow for road traffic to cross. When they were closed, a head of water built up and could be maintained for navigation. Passage through the gate was relatively simple when the upstream and downstream water levels were similar. At other times it could be hazardous and dangerous, boats either being swept rapidly downstream by the torrent flowing through the gate or having to be hauled or winched slowly through the cascading water.

Whilst these sluices theoretically enabled navigation, in practice it was difficult as the mill owners still considered they had first right to the water. Unless there was some specific, generally financial, arrangement with the miller, no boat was allowed through the sluices, the millers claiming that by passing water through the sluices, "there will not be sufficient [water] to grind such corn or grain as there shall be occasion to grind".

There followed almost immediately a conflict, which continues today, between navigation and flood prevention. The miller at Godmanchester was empowered to open all the sluices whenever there was even the smallest risk of a flood. As long as there was sufficient water for his mill, he did this, in all probability, as often as possible in order to disrupt the navigation. The problem is somewhat different today. It centres around the question "Are the locks and sluices provided primarily for navigation or flood control?". There is no doubt that whilst they were installed originally for navigation, if they had not been there, it could be argued that they would not have impeded flood flow. However, they were there and because they impeded flood flows they had to be adapted to provide, additionally, for flood control. The question of payment for the combined structures then arose; should the considerable costs be paid by the navigators or those who benefited from the flood defences? Because the navigators could not afford the total costs, a generally acceptable compromise was reached whereby the navigators paid for the lock pens and the doors, whilst the sluices were financed, with central government support, by those who benefited from the flood protection provided.

As the river meanders in a very wide floodplain, forming large meadows, William Cowper's "spacious meads", it passes Wyton, Houghton, and the Hemingfords.

In Wyton, The Three Jolly Butchers Public House, with its river-side garden, was once a yeoman farmer's house. Dating from 1622, there are some early decorative wall paintings believed to have been drawn in the early 17th century with animal's blood. Close by a small lane leads to the sad, redundant church of St Margaret and All Saints. Closed in 1974 and partially converted to a dwelling by the comedienne Ruby Wax, it dates from the early 13th century, and was where Charles James Fox married Elizabeth Blane on 28 September 1795. Born in 1749, Fox became a Member of Parliament when he was only 19. In spite of living a rakish and dissipated life during which he threw away a fortune on gambling and cards, he was a very eloquent speaker. For twenty years he opposed William Pitt the Younger, supporting unpopular causes such as the French Revolution, injustice in Ireland and corruption in India. He championed the movement against the slave trade. Following William Pitt's death, he returned to office and just before he died in 1806, passed his motion for the abolition of the slave trade.

In the tended graveyard are 27 of graves of airmen from the Royal Flying Corps, the Royal Air Force, the Royal Canadian Air Force and the Royal Australian Air Force who had been stationed at RAF Wyton and who were killed during the First and Second World Wars. Although some distance from the river, the airfield was first opened on 27 March 1918. It was used for training flights, one of which crashed into the spire of St Ives parish church; half the spire was demolished and the pilot killed. In between the First and Second World Wars the land reverted to agricultural use, only to be reopened as an airfield on 30 July 1936. It was from here at one minute past noon on 3 September 1939, only 61 minutes after war between England and Germany had been declared, that the first operational sortie of the war took place. It was a reconnaissance flight by Blenheim 6215 to photograph warships in the German North Sea near Wilhelmshaven. This was the first of many flights of a force which became established in 1942 as the Pathfinder Force. Not only did the first operational flight of the war take off from RAF Wyton, but also bombers from the station took part in the last Bomber Command sortie of the war on 2/3 May 1945. Reconnaissance continued and in 1953, the Photographic Reconnaissance Unit was formed using Valiant, Victor and Canberra aircraft, a far cry from the early Shorthorns, Avros and Sopwith Camels. Three of the remaining Canberras formed the fly-past when the station was closed from operational flying in 1994.

Houghton immediately adjoins Wyton and was the home of the miller Potto Brown (1797-1871), where he "spent his life devoting himself to the best interests of those around him". Related to the Browns of Earith, he was know locally as the "village philanthropist". Coming from a Quaker family, he was an extraordinary man with very narrow religious views, indeed he was disowned by the Quakers in 1837. He was guided by his "lights" to do good works and it is said that in times of financial difficulty he would take his ledgers to church seeking help from God by telling Him who owed him money. He prayed that he might be "acute in business, successful at market and able to make money". He was also an inventor and made a number of changes to ensure the efficient running of Houghton Mill, which he rented from Lady Olivia Bernard Sparrow of Brampton.

For over 1000 years there has been a mill at Houghton. In 974, Earldorman Aylwin, founder of the Benedictine Ramsey Abbey, bought a meadow and mill at Houghton and gave them to the abbey as a part of its endowment, the miller's tolls forming part of the abbey's income. In 1086 the value of the mill was 20 shillings and by 1165 this had increased to 100 shillings. Its economic viability was ensured because, under the threat of a severe fine, all the tenants of lands belonging to Ramsey Abbey were required to have their corn ground at Houghton. Following the Dissolution of the Monasteries in 1539, the mill was seized and owned by the Crown until 1625 when it was sold by Charles 1 to the Duke of Manchester, who in turn sold it to Robert Bernard of Brampton Hall in 1651. It passed to Lady Olivier Bernard Sparrow when she was widowed in 1805. After a succession of owners and tenants it was closed in 1920. In 1939 it was given to the National Trust and then leased until 1983 to the Youth Hostels Association. A lengthy period of restoration culminated in 1999 with the completion of a joint National Trust and Environment Agency venture costing £1.2m and within which a water-wheel was re-installed, a hydro-electric turbine installed and improvements to the flood defence sluices carried out.

On the south side of the river, "The Hemingfords", Hemingford Abbots and Hemingford Grey, originated as one settlement, Hemingford, the Ford of Hema's People. In the 11th century, 18 hides of land to the west of the settlement were granted by King Hardecanute to Ramsey Abbey and the remainder of the manor, 11 hides, was then granted by William the Conqueror to Aubrey de Vere. (A "hide" was a measure of land reckoned to be large enough to support a family and its dependants, generally between 60 and 120 acres [OED]). The de Veres were eventually succeeded in the middle of the 13th century, by Sir John de Grey, Justice of Chester. He became Lord of the Manor through his marriage, without royal licence in 1251, to Emma de Cauz, heiress to the manor. Hence the two parts of Hemingford gradually became known as Hemingford Abbots and Hemingford Grey.

After the Dissolution of the Monasteries, the manor of Hemingford Abbots passed through a number of hands including the Duke of Northumberland, Sir Thomas Seymore, and the Marchioness of Northampton. In the mid-17th century it was divided into two, half being acquired, along with its mill, by Robert Bernard, the owner of Houghton Mill.

The two manors of Hemingford Abbots and Hemingford Grey became united again in 1727, under James Mitchell of Fowlmere. The riverside Manor House in Hemingford Grey, surrounded on three sides by a moat and dating from about 1130, is reputedly the oldest inhabited house in England. Typical of a Norman house, it was built in two stories, the upper comprising the living quarters entered at first floor level by an external flight of steps. Despite extensive alterations in the 16th century, and a terrible fire in the 18th century, original windows and the entrance, now also a window, remain.

(See colour section for larger photo)

Of all the families that have lived there, two are of particular interest. The first is James Gunning's family. Originally from Castlecoot in Ireland and related to the Mitchells, James was the lessee of the Manor House in about 1730. He had four daughters; the two youngest, Maria and Elizabeth were born respectively in 1733 and 1734. The two sisters were to become much admired society beauties. Each were married clandestinely into the aristocracy in 1752; Maria to George, sixth Earl of Coventry and Elizabeth, to James, sixth Duke of Hamilton. Elizabeth's marriage, after she had eloped, took place at midnight on St Valentine's day in Mayfair Chapel without banns, licence or a traditional ring, a bedside curtain ring being used instead of the real thing. The Duke of Hamilton died in 1758 and a year later Elizabeth married John Campbell, the Marquess of Lorne and future fourth Duke of Argyle. Not only did she marry two Dukes, becoming both a Baroness and a Duchess, but before she died in 1790 she had become mother to four Dukes!

Her marriage, however, created such an immediate scandal which led to the introduction of Earl Hardwicke's Marriage Act of 1753. It was designed to prevent such marriages, and gave rise to the introduction of new church registers, invaluable to genealogists.

The second family could hardly be more of a contrast. In 1939, the Manor was bought by Lucy Boston, the author of the famous "Green Knowe" children's stories, written in the 1950s. It was to be her home until she died in 1990 aged 97. The Manor House, with its unique timeless atmosphere, and its garden, became in effect, Green Knowe. It had been the home of a fictional group of 17th century children who had befriended a little boy, Tolly, and his great-grandmother, Old Mrs Oldknow, who had come to live there. When Tolly returned to school after his holidays at Green Knowe, he asked "Why do people only invent things that go faster and faster, instead of finding some way to keep it at now?". Whoever built the Manor House knew the answer to that question.

Lucy Boston was not only an author. During the Second World War she gave gramophone recitals to air crew from RAF Wyton, a tradition continued through the summer concerts held in a beautiful, scented, riverside garden which she had filled with sweet briar, honeysuckle, pinks, lavenders, lilacs, and irises. Above all she loved scented roses and planted over 300 traditional varieties, all bred before 1900, including red-purple Rose du Roi, ruby-red Conditorium, Tudor damask roses and the fuchsia-red Rose De Rescht, which may date to Roman times. In the winter, when she could not work in the garden, she designed and made exquisite patchwork quilts. Not only did she make patchworks by the fire, but so did Old Mrs Oldknow.

From the garden, where children still laugh, there is an unforgettable view of St James' parish church, a church to which William Cowper's description of Hartford church could equally apply. Dating from the 13th century, its spire was blown down during the great gale of 8th September 1741. According to a local legend, a swineherd visited a nearby company of Grey Friars who, with their Cardinal Gull'em, were feasting and drinking. The swineherd asked the cardinal to come and give the last rights to his dying master. On entering the house, the Cardinal was confronted by the Devil, who said, that whilst he was pleased with what Gull'em had done, he was to damn from the pulpit all those whose views were not held by the Pope. If he did not, the Devil would visit the church and fly off with the steeple. One can only assume the Cardinal did not do as he was asked!

Round yet another meadow are the western outskirts of St Ives. Indeed St Ives probably started life here as a small Saxon village called Slepe. In AD 986 the head of the local Saxon family, Mannesonne, died, bequeathing his Manor to Ramsey Abbey in whose jurisdiction it was to remain for the next 500 years. Some 14 or 15 years later these monks were to come to a conclusion which was to have quite an impact on Slepe. Having been called to examine a stone coffin containing a skeleton which had been unearthed when a field to the east of Slepe was being ploughed, they immediately attributed the body to a 7th century Persian Bishop, the by-then canonised St Ivo. A small priory was built on the site in 1017 and the bones removed to a shrine at Ramsey Abbey. Apart from some stone walling, no trace remains of the priory, which was dissolved in 1539. However, by that date the town of St Ives had become well established between the priory to the east and Slepe to the west.

Quite why the monks should have assumed that the body was that of St Ivo is not clear. Perhaps it was a ruse to promote trade through his sanctity and reputed healing powers. Whatever the reasons, the body was almost certainly that of a Roman farmer who had lived in a Roman villa whose remains were discovered in 1981, under the site of the former priory. If it was a ruse, it worked; pilgrims arrived, trade increased, the monks developed St Ives, in about 1107 a wooden bridge was built to replace the old ford and in 1110 Henry 1 granted a charter for an annual Easter Fair, a fair which was to become one of the largest fairs in England.

In 1414 the monks agreed to replace the wooden bridge with a stone bridge of six arches. During the Civil War, the Roundheads replaced the southern arches with a wooden drawbridge. Subsequent rebuilding in 1717 did not retain the original style and round arches replaced the original pointed arches. It carried a small stone chapel which was consecrated in 1426 and dedicated to St Ledger. This chapel has had many uses: it was used by the monks not only for services but also as a toll house, following the Dissolution of the Monasteries in 1539, it was the home of the former prior, in 1736 it was turned into a private house and two storeys were added, and it was an inn having a somewhat dubious reputation, locally known as "Little Hell". The chapel was restored to its original condition in 1930 and the bridge completely refurbished in 2000.

St Ives had a non-conformist tradition, which no doubt suited Oliver Cromwell, farmer and townsman of St Ives between 1631 and 1636. To mark the tercentenary of his birth, a statue in his memory was offered to the Burgesses of Huntingdon, his birthplace. Whilst they refused to accept the statue, it was readily accepted in St Ives. Made of bronze and standing on a Portland stone plinth, it was erected in 1901. One of a very small number of statues of Oliver Cromwell, it is an impressive statue which depicts him striding imperiously down the Market Place, bible under one arm and wearing an enormous hat.

He would have known Dr. Robert Wilde (1609 to 1679), puritan, poet and minister of the parish church. He must have enjoyed making his will under which, once a year he was able to turn the altar into a gaming table. He required that 12 children, six boys and six girls, "such as are good and of good report, all born in the parish, each above the age of 12 years and everyone able to read the bible" be selected to dice for Bibles.

His will which enabled this practice said that "upon the Whitsun Tuesday before morning prayer, after the sermon bell is rung, the minister and officers and other grave townsmen being also present, the minister in a few words praying to God to direct the lots to His glory, let a saucer with three dice be prepared upon the table, [altar] and, beginning with the males, let one bible be cast for by each pair and the party who casts the greater number at one cast have that bible, and so two by two until all be cast for". The bibles were bought through a bequest made by Dr. Wilde of £50 to buy land, which became known as Bible Orchard, and which would give an income of £3 per year. Play still takes place, but on a table, not the altar.

A short distance downstream from St Ives is the small oval village of Holywell. It is an ancient village and possibly, like St Ives, it grew up as a settlement between the church to the west and a ferry, with its ancient inn, to the east. Whilst the present church of St John the Baptist dates from the end of the 12th century, there is evidence that a church existed here in the 10th century. Indeed the well, or more accurately spring, at the bottom of the hill by the church and which is credited with healing properties, owes its reputed sanctity to St Ivo. The brick canopy surrounding the well, built in 1845, is dressed and blessed on the Friday nearest 24 June, the festival of St John the Baptist.

At the other end of the village was another ferry, which was probably in use from ancient times until the 1930s. Allegedly Hereward the Wake was one of the passengers and before him perhaps, St Ivo. At such a significant river crossing, a settlement would have been established, no doubt with an "inn". There is evidence of sales of liquor here as early as 560 and some say that the foundations of the Old Ferry Boat Inn are a century older. All this supports the Inn's claim to be "England's Oldest Inn" and it still retains its ancient rights to operate a ferry.

Such ancient sites have their ghosts and the Old Ferry Boat is no exception. According to tradition, a beautiful young seventeen year old girl, Juliet Tewsley, hung herself in 1050 at a nearby cross-roads for the unrequited love of a local woodcutter. A large slab of granite on the floor of the public bar of the Inn is her tombstone. It is said that on the anniversary of her death, March 17th, St Patrick's Day, she walks from her grave to the cross-roads where she died.

The village that has grown up between the church and the Old Ferry Boat Inn provides the first indication of the nearby Fenland rivers. A number of the houses are timber framed dating from the 17th century, some of which were built by Dutch settlers working with Cornelius Vermuyden.

Before reaching these rivers there was one more ferry crossing, again marked by an inn, The Pike and Eel at Overcote. Whilst it is known to have operated from the mid-16th century to about 1900, it is likely that this too was an ancient crossing. Oliver Cromwell is said to have frequented the inn and in one of the original rooms is a hidden trap door said to have been used as an escape route. Like the Ferry Boat, it too has its ghost. According to the legend, it is that of a maid who Cromwell killed by pushing her down the stairs after he had discovered her eavesdropping on one of his meetings.

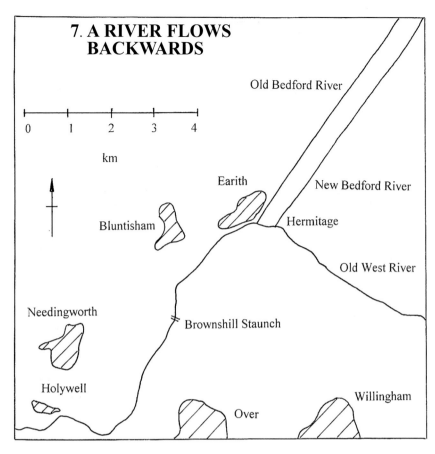

7. A RIVER FLOWS BACKWARDS

Old Bedford River

0   1   2   3   4

km

Earith

New Bedford River

Bluntisham

Hermitage

Old West River

Needingworth

Brownshill Staunch

Holywell

Willingham

Over

So the river flows across the Greenwich Meridian to Brownshill Staunch. To all intents and purposes, Brownshill Staunch, dating from 1834, looks just like any other lock and flood control structure with its lock pen, pair of large vertical lift gates to cope with both fluvial and tidal flows and, at the side, three radial flood gates. Here the river starts its journey across the Fens, leaving behind its natural "sinuous course" for ever. Here 62km from the open sea, three important and interdependent changes occur. The river becomes tidal, it starts to cross the low-lying fenland and for the rest of its course to the sea, is mostly man-made. To understand the reasons for these changes, a brief account of the history of Fenland is necessary.

Between 100 million and 40 million years ago, during the Cretaceous period, the North Sea covered much of East Anglia and North West Europe and in this vast basin, deposits of clay and chalk were laid down on the underlying Jurassic clay. Then, as a result of earth movements, these deposits were gradually raised well above sea level to form one huge land mass, across which the predecessors of the East Anglian rivers, the River Thames and the River Rhine flowed north and east. Over a long period these rivers gradually eroded the chalk away to form great river basins, of which the Wash is a remnant. The Jurassic clays were exposed again and a slightly undulating landscape was formed with scattered outliers of less resistant rocks, which would later form the Fenland "Islands".

Some 18 thousand years ago during the latter part of the Pleistocene period, much of this landscape was covered again when the last great ice sheet reached its southern-most limit. About 8 thousand years later, as the weather improved, the ice retreated and melted. Not only did the basins emerge again, largely unaltered except for a capping of Boulder Clay on the higher "Islands", but sea level rose by up to 100m and East Anglia began to tilt slowly downwards. The British Isles thus became separated from north-west Europe, the sea flooded into part of the East Anglian river basin to form the Wash and the remainder of the basin was poised to become today's Fenland.

There then followed a long and very complicated process of silt and clay deposition in the inland basin. Initially the tides brought in marine silts which were deposited at the seaward edge of the basin. As these deposits rose, salt marsh plants became established, causing further silt deposition. Thus a ridge of higher land gradually became established around the coastal rim of the basin and it became increasingly difficult for the silt laden inland rivers to reach the sea. So not only did they deposit their silt along the river valleys but also, because of long and frequent periods of fresh water flooding, they deposited them over a very wide area behind the coastal rim. Trees and plants soon became established inland. As all these plants decayed, the first peat was formed.

Although the major changes had been brought about by the melting ice caps, there were two more periods when the land was covered again by the sea. The first was between 6 thousand and 4 thousand years ago and a layer of silt and clay, The Barroway Beds, was deposited. This killed the underlying vegetation, which, as it decayed, added more peat to the early deposits. Once the silts and clays had risen above the mean tide level, vegetation became established again and as it in turn decayed, another extensive layer of peat, the Nordelph Peat, was formed. The second time the land was covered by the sea was about 2 thousand years ago and the process was more or less repeated. This time, however, the layer of silt and clay, The Terrington Beds, was deposited not only over much of the Barroway Beds and the northern part of the Nordelph Peat, but also, because the strong tidal flow overcame the much weaker fresh water flow, along the river valleys.

Whilst in general East Anglia was slowly tilting seawards, there were times when this was reversed. When the land was sinking, clay was deposited in the deeper waters of northern Fenland and the tidal silts were not only deposited further inland, but they were also carried far up the rivers onto whose beds they were then deposited. Fresh water thus found its way to the sea becoming increasingly choked and so it flooded, with its load of silt, over southern Fenland. When the land was rising, the gradient to the sea became so shallow that again the fresh water could not escape and so it continued to flood, but this time over a much greater area. The maze of sluggish watercourses and lagoons through which the water tried to escape to the sea was ideal for plant growth and the formation of marshes, which, when they decayed gave rise to more peat deposits.

Thus Fenland, a low-lying often waterlogged peaty and silty land with a myriad of watercourses, meres and swamps interspersed with a few "islands" of dry land, gradually evolved. Whilst it is very difficult to describe the drainage associated with these geological events, a very general picture can be derived from a series of clues.

Fresh water silts, sands and gravels were deposited not only on the beds of these early rivers, but also, as they flooded, on their banks like levees. These were less easily compressed than the surrounding softer clays and winding ridges, known as "Roddons" or "Rodhams", emerged, mirroring the rivers' and streams' courses. They provide one of the best means of tracing the ancient rivers and despite years of weathering, drainage and agricultural working, many are visible today, showing up either as prominent ridges standing proud of the surrounding land, as bands of lighter coloured silty, sandy soil which contrast with the surrounding darker peat, or as bands where the growth and colour of the vegetation has been affected. Some of the best examples of "Roddons" in the country can be seen between Ely and Stuntney and criss-crossing the road between Littleport and Mildenhall, marking the early course of the rivers Great Ouse and Little Ouse respectively.

Again, because they were made up of relatively hard, incompressible materials, they have been frequently used since Roman times, as foundations for roads, farms, houses, churches, villages and even modern housing estates. Thus sinuous roads, lanes, footpaths or lines of houses often mark an ancient river's course, as for example between Somersham and Chatteris, or at Welney, reflecting ancient western and eastern channels of the River Great Ouse respectively and apparently out-lying farms can be linked together by a common, but now extinct, river.

There are other clues. These early watercourses, some of which still exist today as rivers, streams or ditches, formed natural boundaries, which over time became established as administrative boundaries. The Norfolk and Cambridgeshire County Council boundary between Welney and Upwell follows for much of the way, a small stream, the Old Croft River, which is itself all that remains of the ancient Welney River or Wellstream, the major eastern channel of the River Great Ouse.

There is documentary and scientific evidence. Whilst the Anglo Saxon Chronicle makes early references to fens, rivers and meres, the map makers of the late-16th and early-17th century produced very detailed maps. Their representation of the rivers is remarkably close to that revealed from modern geological and soil surveys.

Before man's influence, the pattern of the rivers was very different to that which exists today. Whilst some modern river and place names are used, for ease of interpretation the River Great Ouse has been treated as having three sections; Western, Eastern and Northern. At Earith, some 4km downstream from Brownshill Staunch, the River Great Ouse was joined from the east by a tributary, the Aldreth or Old West River. The combined rivers flowed north for about 2km before dividing into two streams, the principal one of which was called the West Water (the Western Ouse), and flowed generally north west towards Benwick, where they not only rejoined but were also joined from the west by a precursor to the River Nene. This large river, made up of the Old River Nene and the Western Ouse, then flowed past March and through Outwell, to the sea, then at Wisbech.

Another upland river, the River Cam (the Eastern Ouse), flowed north from Cambridge past Stretham, where it was joined from the west by a small but important tributary. Its early course was well to the east of Ely and after a series of meanders it was joined by two further rivers, the forerunners of the Rivers Lark and Little Ouse. These combined rivers, then called the Wellstream, or Wellenhee (the Eastern Ouse), flowed north west across the Fens past Littleport and Welney where they were joined by yet another tributary, the upland part of which was the River Wissey. It met the Old River Nene and the Western Ouse at Outwell and so also flowed into the sea at Wisbech.

To complete the picture of those rivers which would play a part in the development of the River Great Ouse as we know it today, the ancient River Nar flowed east to Wiggenhall where it met a tributary flowing in from the south (the Northern Ouse). After two great loops which turned the river through nearly 180 degrees and back again, it flowed out to the sea at King's Lynn. This river and the River Gaywood, were the only rivers at that time to reach the sea at this point. All the others flowed to the sea at Wisbech.

The stage was now set for mankind to intervene. Whilst Iron Age man settled around the edge of the fens, he did not penetrate further. It was the Romans who were amongst the first to realise the potential wealth that could be gained from cultivating the fen soils. They built a road from Swaffham and the Devil's Dyke to Denver and thence, lying on the old silts, right across the fens to Peterborough.

However, their most ambitious work was the construction of the Car Dyke, primarily a waterway for navigation, part natural and part artificial, linking Cambridge to Peterborough and Lincoln. The route initially followed the River Cam to a spot between Horningsea and Clayhythe where a canal was built linking the River Cam with the West Water. It continued along the West Water to Benwick and beyond to Peterborough.

It is almost certain that they carried out a number of other works which would have a major impact on the river system. When they were building the Car Dyke, it is likely that they also joined the eastern tributary of the West Water with the small tributary that flowed into the Eastern Ouse at Stretham, thus linking the Western Ouse directly with the Eastern Ouse. They probably diverted the Wellstream (the Eastern Ouse) at Littleport, north to join the River Little Ouse, which they had already straightened to a more northerly course, and beyond through Nordelph to the Northern Ouse. At the same time it is most likely that they joined a small tributary running east from Outwell to the small river at Nordelph and so also into the Northern Ouse. This became known as Well Creek.

After the Romans left, their works gradually fell into disrepair and the next significant period to impact on the fens was that of the great monastic building which started in the middle of the 7th century. Many of the churches, abbeys, monasteries, and cathedrals built both in and around the fens, were constructed of Barnack Stone quarried from near Peterborough, much of which would have been transported by water.

Whether the many works attributed to the Romans were actually carried out by them or were as a consequence of the monastic building will probably never be known. What is certain, however, is that by the 13th century, the Western Ouse from Earith had become almost extinct, the majority of the water from the River Great Ouse flowed east from Earith to the Eastern Ouse at Stretham. At Littleport, whilst the majority of the flow went directly north past Nordelph to the Northern Ouse and to the sea at King's Lynn, there was some flow along the Wellstream to Outwell. Here it was joined by the River Nene and it then flowed back to the Northern Ouse at Nordelph via Well Creek. The net effect was that the whole of the flow of the River Great Ouse and a significant proportion of the flow of the River Nene reached the sea at King's Lynn as opposed to Wisbech.

Drainage works which were started in the Fens during the late-15th century laid down the principals for the major drainage works of the 17th century, namely that straightening up the watercourses would speed up their flow. It was not until the 17th century, however, that it was realised by Sir Robert Bevill, that another ingredient was required; drainage had to be on a regional, and not local, scale.

In 1630, a group of landowners approached Francis 4th Earl of Bedford to drain the whole of southern Fenland in return for 38,500ha of land. Of this 16,200ha would be taxed to meet operating costs, 4,900ha were to be allocated to the King and the remaining 17,400ha were for the investors. Thirteen business men, known as "Adventurers" because they "adventured" their capital joined the Earl and they appointed Cornelius Vermuyden to drain the "Great Level of the Fens".

He had been born in St Maartensdijk, a town in the province of Zeeland in the Netherlands, probably in 1590 and was the son of a long established family. Quite why he was called to England in 1621 to assist the Dutch drainage engineer Joachim Liens is not clear. There is no record of his professional experience and at the time he was working as a tax collector. Never the less, he and his family must have been highly respected and talented for him to be entrusted with important drainage undertakings in England.

His first major undertaking was to drain Hatfield Chase, Yorkshire in 1626. Whilst he based this work on the sound principles of straightening the natural winding rivers and providing washlands, it was to prove to be not entirely a technical success. Although some areas benefited greatly, it was at the expense of others and it was a financial disaster for all the participants. He became unpopular and where those works had adversely affected the commoners, there were riots and even loss of life. Never the less he was Knighted for these works in 1629 and his technical reputation was established.

His initial terms of reference for the drainage of the "Great Level of the Fens" were somewhat ambiguous, but he understood that he was to make summer farming reliable and to prevent serious, but not all, winter flooding. The major work he carried out during this period of his employment was the construction of the Bedford River completed in 1637 and which ran in a straight line from a new sluice at Earith to another new sluice on the River Great Ouse near Denver. At the same time he straightened the route between Ely and Littleport, shortening it by about 20km. Initially these works were thought to have achieved the terms of reference, however, within a couple of years Vermuyden received further instructions to carry out works which would enable year-round farming.

Works were started immediately, only to be interrupted by the Civil War in 1642. They were started again in 1649 and three works were to have an even greater effect on the River Great Ouse. First, he cut another new river, The Hundred Foot Drain or New Bedford River running parallel to the first (now Old) Bedford River directly to the River Great Ouse at Denver. Secondly, he built great Barrier banks along the outer banks of the two Bedford Rivers. Thirdly, he built a new sluice at Denver to prevent both the tide and the flow from the Bedford Rivers from flowing back along the Great Ouse.

The net effect was that by 1652, upland water could not only be conveyed from Earith directly to Denver, but in times of flood could flow through a sluice into the Old Bedford River and instead of spreading over the neighbouring Fenland, flood onto the vast reservoir, 2,270ha, lying between the two barrier banks. It was accepted that the aims had now been achieved.

Although Vermuyden died in 1677, that was not to be the end of his works. His original plans of 1640 envisaged a "Cut Off Channel" which in times of flood would intercept and draw off water from the surrounding higher land before it entered the Fenland and transfer it to a "Relief Channel" running from Denver to the sea, parallel to the River Great Ouse, but in a straight line. After many years of controversy concerning the efficacy of Denver Sluice, Sir Murdoch MacDonald and Partners proposed in 1940 that a "Relief Channel" be built to take flood water from Denver directly to an outfall at St Germans near King's Lynn. Not only did the war intervene but the 1947 Flood demonstrated that this work in itself would have been insufficient to prevent the flooding that had occurred. The original scheme was revised in 1954 and a "Cut Off Channel" included. The work was finished in 1964, and the two new rivers followed virtually the same course Vermuyden had proposed some 324 years earlier.

Vermuyden's involvement with the drainage of the fens finished in February 1655, some 34 years after his first appointment. According to the register of St Margaret's Church, Westminster, where he is buried, he died in October 1677 aged 87. The lower stretches of the River Great Ouse will remain as his most remarkable legacy.

I sing Floods muzled and the Ocean tam'd
Luxurious Rivers govern'd and reclam'd
Water with Banks confined as in a Gaol
Till kinder Sluices let them go on bail.
Streams curb'd with Dammes like Bridles
taught t'obey
And run as strait, as if they saw their way.

Samuel Fortrey (1685).

Below the sluice and to the north of the river is Bluntisham. Its former rectory, a restored Queen Anne building and whose doorway came from the old Slepe Hall in St Ives, became Dorothy Sayers' home when her father, Henry Sayers, became rector of the Bluntisham cum Earith parish church of St Mary in 1897. Born in 1893 and educated at the Godolphin School and Somerville College, Oxford, she became one of the best known English crime writers. Her novels featured Lord Peter Wimsey, his "right hand man" Bunter and her heroine Harriet Vane. One in particular, a fascinating novel about campanology, The Nine Tailors (1934), was set in Fenland. Whilst she may have drawn on experiences from her early life in Bluntisham Rectory, the setting is more likely to be in and around the small Parish of Christchurch in the Fens near March, after her father had swapped parishes in 1918.

The parish church has a magnificent raised site to the north of the present river, which prior to the fen drainage works ran close by the small hill on which the church stands. Dating from the early 14th century, it has a unique three sided apse and a very tall spire visible for miles.

Below the church and close to the present main road, which again prior to the fen drainage works had simply been a causeway from the church to Earith, is a small stream, probably a remnant of the ancient river. On a small promontory nearby, farmed by Richard Brown, a local farmer and landlord who lived in Earith High Street, a small bronze Romano-Gallic statue of a warrior was found in 1826. There is no clear consensus of opinion as to who is actually represented. Some say it is a Jupiter Martialis, some say it is a Mars Ultor and yet others believe it is of Emperor Commodus playing the role of Hercules-Mars. The somewhat fearsome statue is clad in gladiatorial costume and the Roman Emperor Lucius Commodus (161-192) was certainly a violent man known to be a tyrant who enjoyed murder and gladiatorial combats. Indeed he met his death by strangulation, instigated by his mistress and others who found themselves on his death list.

(See colour section for larger photo)

The spot where he was found overlooks a sweep of land running down to the river bank, known as Little or Berry or Bury Fen, for many years one of the homes of the Fen Skating Championships and the birth place of "Bandy", not a person but a game. A 19th century description of Fenland skaters describes them as powerful broad-backed men, with a slow, heavy, almost stiff, gait. "Although on land they could run half a mile, yet on ice, with only a day's practice, they can hold their own and beat the best trained skaters of the world". The famous Welney skaters, "Turkey" Smart, "Fish" Smart and "Gutta Percha" See and the Tebbutt brothers from Bluntisham, all with their low crouching style, their heads almost level with their knees and arms either behind their backs on the straights or swinging wildly round the corners, all skated on Bury Fen.

Tebbutt said that "If Lords Ground is associated with cricket, then Bury Fen may claim to be the home, if not the birth place of Bandy"; Bandy, the fore-runner of ice hockey. The game has been played on the fen for more than 150 years and Bluntisham and Earith had a run of 100 years when they did not suffer a defeat. Even today whenever the ice freezes, generally after three nights of a hard frost and low daytime temperatures, some form of "Bandy" is played.

There was a very different scene in March 1947. The preceding winter had been very severe with heavy snow fall throughout eastern England. On 10th March the snow turned to heavy rain and a rapid thaw started. Generally it takes about three days for upland waters to reach Earith and sure enough on 13 March the river started to rise, not smoothly as it does now, but in sudden rushes as the flood overcame poorly maintained structures or stretches. During the night of 16th/17th March when the river was at the peak of its flood and when there were severe gales, the Barrier Bank opposite Bury Fen, breached. Billions of gallons of water poured through a 50m gap in the bank flooding thousands of acres of land in what was described as "possibly the greatest flood since the fens were first drained". The army was called in to seal the breach. Under the code name "Operation Neptune", a dam made of Neptune amphibious vehicles was made around the breach, which could then be rebuilt and resealed.

Earith, meaning a muddy landing place, had a relatively high level of commercial prosperity as evidenced by a number of fine early 19th century houses. Of the many wharves and warehouses, little now remains, however incorporated in the gardens of a modern riverside estate are the remains of wharves and kilns built by John Jewson, son of George Jewson who, in 1836, had founded the business of Jewson and Sons, Builders Merchants. Much of the timber and the chalk (clunch) for making lime was brought in by barge from King's Lynn in Norfolk and Isleham in Suffolk respectively. Whilst in 1868 new premises had been found in Norwich and Yarmouth, Jewsons retained a yard in Earith until November 1989.

At the eastern edge of the village are the three radial flood control gates leading to the Old Bedford River. In 1637 there were nine holes (gates), in 1824, seven holes and in 1954, three holes. Close by is an RAF memorial, erected in November 1999. "On 17 January 1942 Stirling Aircraft W7467 of 7 Squadron RAF flying from RAF Oakington collided with a Hurricane Aircraft of No 56 OTU and crashed 1.5 miles north of Earith. All (7) crew members were killed".

Between the Old Bedford River and New Bedford River are earthworks called The Bulwarks. The nature of their origin is unclear. Some say that they were Roman, however no artefacts have been found. There is a reference in Camden's Britannia (1580), to fortresses being built at "Earyth" and "Althred" during the time of William the Conqueror. A likely theory is that it was one of several such forts built to protect the river crossings and causeways across the Fens, in this case Earith Causeway, the first known reference to Earith Causeway being in 1150, (Aldreth is the site of another fenland causeway). So, if not Roman, it is likely that the fortifications date from at least the late 11th century. However, the present form of the Bulwarks, a square fort with bastions at the corners, dates from Cromwellian times and it was one of several which guarded the roads and causeways from Huntingdonshire into Cambridgeshire and across the fens.

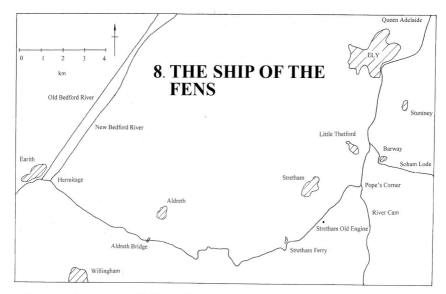

8. THE SHIP OF THE FENS

It was the responsibility of the Bishops of Ely to maintain the river crossing at Earith and the causeway leading to Ely. Whilst they were very quick to charge a toll for crossing, they were not good at keeping the crossings in good repair. Indeed in 1286 the crossings were in such a bad state that they became impassable and the sheriff was ordered to carry out repairs at the Bishop's cost. In spite of this, 60 years later they were in a complete state of decay and again the Bishop was ordered to carry out repairs. By the late 14th century the Bishop had installed a hermit at Earith to repair and maintain the bridge and causeway. Although there is no trace of either the hermitage in which he lived or of the adjoining small chapel dedicated to St Mary, Hermitage Lock commemorates, through its name, the hermits of Earith.

A lock separating the River Great Ouse and the New Bedford River from the Old West River, has been in existence in some form or other since the mid-17th century. It generally prevents the River Great Ouse from flowing to the sea in the very long, circuitous inland route past Ely and Littleport, and forces it to take the shorter, direct route via the tidal New Bedford River.

It also maintains a large reservoir of water, sometimes called the El Pond, contained in the River Great Ouse (Ely Ouse) and fed by the River Cam, Lark, Little Ouse, and Wissey. It was to play a key role during the drought of 1976 when East Anglia in particular was facing severe wate supply restrictions. Engineers from Anglian Water had spent long day looking for ways in which the dwindling supplies held in Grafham Wate could be replenished. Of the many very original ideas discussed, some sa late at night in a local pub, one, on reflection, proved to be a realistic innovative and somewhat risky solution.

The volume of water coming down the River Great Ouse to Earith wa very little. The river was shallow, gradients were very small and what wate there was, was being wasted as it flowed out to the sea along the Ne Bedford River. On the other hand there was a reasonable quantity of wate held in the Ely Pond. The solution was to move this water upstream from th Ely Pond to the intake at Grafham Water. It was achieved by installing larg pumps at Hermitage Lock and all the other locks between Earith and th Grafham Water intake. A temporary dam was built across the New Bedfor River to prevent any escape to the sea. The idea worked and for a short tim the River Great Ouse could be seen flowing backwards.

At the same time the Labour Government appointed Dennis Howell a Minister of Drought. There must be very few times that any Governmer Minister achieved such an instant success. Within a few days of hi appointment, the drought broke, there was heavy rain and, to prever flooding, the dam across the New Bedford River had to be rapidly removec

Hermitage was not only a road crossing. Beside the lock, appearing now to be very incongruous, is a cottage called The Station House, a reminder of the former Ely and St Ives railway which crossed the river here. Under an Act of June 1864, a railway had been constructed from Ely to Sutton via Stretham, Wilburton and Haddenham and opened in April 1865. In 1876 the first move was made by the Great Eastern Railway to extend the railway via Earith and Bluntisham to St Ives. Fully opened on 10 May 1878, it provided not only passenger services, but importantly a goods service for coal, fruit and sugar beet. In 1931 the average time for the 28km journey was 44 minutes. After the Second World War passenger use became limited to excursion trains. These ceased in 1957 and the stretch between Bluntisham and Sutton finally closed on 6 October 1958. This, however, was not to be the end of a local association with railways. In the early 1970s an experimental tracked hovercraft train was developed. The monorail track from Earith ran parallel with the Old Bedford River for about 4km. Although a prototype reached a speed of 107 mph, its potential was never fully realised and the Government scrapped the project in 1974.

From Hermitage Lock, the Old West River initially follows its ancient east west channel in which, at least to begin with, the only flow is as a result of lock openings or land drainage operations. It is a narrow twisting river, prone to heavy weed growth in the summer. After passing a stretch lined with poplar trees and reminiscent of French waterways, it is crossed by the Aldreth Causeway, another major causeway, dating from the Bronze Age, linking the "mainland" with the Isle of Ely. It ran from Willingham in the south, to Aldreth in the north, through Belsar's Hill, a simple round Iron Age or early medieval earthwork traditionally associated with William the Conqueror. Whilst some say it was named after a Norman commander, Belsar, the name "Bellassise" was in use in the 13th century. The latter name may have been sarcastically adopted by the Norman soldiers who earlier had had to serve in this "beautiful seat".

Tradition goes further. The building of the causeway itself is also attributed by some to William, and it is supposed that the great battle of *Alherede, Alrehethe* or between William and Hereward the Wake occurred near the river crossing at Aldreth High Bridge. This tradition may owe much to writers such as those in the 12th century *Liber Eliensis* and the 13th century *De Gestis Herwardi* and more recently, Charles Kingsley, who, in his book *Hereward the Wake*, refers to arms and weapons being found in "that black half mile". Despite many excavations and dredgings, no such artefacts have been found. Not only that, but some of the more contemporary accounts do not match this site in terms of topography and distances, whilst other accounts suggest that Hereward's army actually set fire to the causeway when the Norman army was half-way across. So whilst this causeway may have been one of those used during the attack on Hereward, it is more likely that the main assault was launched across the River Ouse near Stuntney.

To the south of Aldreth High Bridge is Hempsal's Fen, Hempsal's Fen Farm and Hempsal Farm. Could this Fen and these Farms give substance to the legend of a certain farmer Joseph Hempsall? Whilst the legend as told by Christopher Marlowe refers to Hempsall, not Hempsal, and is set between Upware on the River Cam, Wicken and Soham some 10km to the east, it could equally apply to the Old West River, Willingham, Aldreth and Haddenham.

According to the old story, every night Joseph would tramp from his farm, along a short cut across the marsh, to drink beer at an Inn which stood on the present site of the Five Miles From Anywhere No Hurry Inn. One evening around Christmas time, there was a sudden very dense fog. When it was time to go home, many at the Inn tried to dissuade Hempsall from taking his usual short cut. He replied, "I'll never go by road not if the Devil himself were waiting out yonder." So saying he set out across the marsh to his farm.

The fog persisted for three days and nothing was heard of the farmer. On the fourth day when the fog had cleared, a certain Elijah Boggers set out to visit Hempsall's Farm. On his way he met Hempsall walking towards him. He turned without a word and walked beside Elijah all the way back to the farm. Close to the house, Hempsall spoke in a hollow sepulchral tone, "go not in there, my body lies in Big-Bog." He continued, "As I am now so one day wilt thou be. I lost my life in Big-Bog on the first night of the fog. Go to Eaudyke and there wilt thou find my body."

Terrified, Elijah set out for Big-Bog and there he found Joseph's body lying half in and half out of the water. He ran for his life not stopping until he reached the riverside Inn. When he had told his story, a party of men set out for Eaudyke to recover the body but however hard they searched, they could not find it. Suddenly however Hempsall appeared. "Fear not," he said "As I am now so must ye all be. Recover my body from the west side of Big-Bog and bury it in Wicken churchyard." The apparition disappeared and a short time after, the men found the body just as Elijah Boggers had. They carried it to Soham where it was buried. Farmer Hempsall haunts these lonely fens and will not rest until his body is buried in Wicken churchyard. Indeed on some foggy nights his dying agonies can be heard as the waters of the dyke closed his mouth for ever. Such is the stuff of legends.

(See colour section for larger photo)

Some 2km east of Aldreth High Bridge the river suddenly turns north through 90°. Geological evidence suggests that the ancient river divided in two here; the major branch meandering north, east and finally south petering out near Twenty Pence road bridge, and the other very minor branch turning south for a very short distance. It seems most likely that the Roman Car Dyke running from Cambridge, joined the main Old West River via this southern branch at the apex of the bend.

At Twenty Pence road bridge, where the river's ancient course finishes, it continues in a bed of modern river terrace gravels as far as Stretham Ferry road bridge where the ancient river gravels become evident again. Not only is this stretch relatively straight, in comparison with the preceding meandering course, but also these two road crossings lie at the eastern and western boundaries of the ancient river gravels. Whilst the Twenty Pence road, as such, is not an old road, its geological setting and alignment from the southern end of the Car Dyke across the river along Twenty Pence Drove, to Wilburton, Wentworth, Coveney and beyond suggest that it may well follow the route of another prehistoric causeway and road, perhaps not dissimilar to Aldreth Causeway. Stretham Ferry, on the other hand, does lie on the course of an ancient road, the Roman Akeman Street. This evidence supports the theory that the length of river between the two roads is the artificial stretch which joined the Old West River with the eastern tributary leading to the River Cam and which thus necessitated the old ferry crossings at Twenty Pence and Stretham.

Some 2km north east of Stretham Ferry Bridge is Stretham Old Engine. During the seventeenth and eighteenth centuries windmills, known as "engines" were used to drain the fens. They were generally of simple construction. The turning sails drove, via two worm and cog wheels, a scoop wheel, so called because it was fitted with paddles or scoops, which literally pushed the water from a lower to a higher level. By the end of the eighteenth century there were 11 windmill pumps along the Old West River. As the fens were drained and the land levels dropped, despite using windmills in pairs to provide a double lift, the wind pumps became a less and less efficient means of draining the fens. Proposals to use steam power were introduced during the 1780s and 1790s. These proposals were slow to be adopted, but eventually, in 1817, the first steam pumping engine was installed near Wisbech. It was successful and as the idea caught on, the wind pumps were quickly replaced with steam powered engines which, with their brick buildings and tall chimneys, changed the face of the fens.

These Fens have oft times been by *Water* drown'd.
Science a remedy in *Water* found.
The powers of *Steam* she said shall be employ'd
And the *Destroyer* by *itself* destroy'd.

Of five steam engines along the Old West River, the preserved Stretham Old Engine is the last. It was built in 1831 to drain 2,500ha of fenland into the Old West River. The original steam engine was a 60hp Boulton and Watt double acting, rotating beam engine which drove a scoop wheel of 8.8m diameter. As the fens continued to shrink, not only were larger scoop wheels installed, 10m in 1850 and 11.3m in 1896, but the engine size was increased to 106hp in 1909. At that date the scoop wheel was fitted with 48 scoops, driven at 4rpm lifting 30 tonnes of water per revolution, whilst the engine consumed 5 tonnes of coal per day.

The age of steam pumping and scoop wheels was however relatively short, since to a certain extent they had become victims of their own success. Due to their efficient drainage of the fens, further shrinkage occurred and scoop wheels were no longer a practical solution. In the 1920s the steam pumps were superseded by diesel pumps which in turn were superseded by electric pumps. At Stretham Engine, although the steam pumps remained operable until 1941, diesel pumps were installed in 1925 and electric pumps in 1943. As with the demise of the windmills, the demise of the steam pumping engines with their tall chimneys and the advent of the diesel and electric pumping stations housed in small brick buildings, changed the Fenland landscape yet again.

So the river continues north east, once again in an ancient channel, to be joined at Pope's Corner by its major tributary the River Cam. On its way it passes through some of the most productive black peat fen soils in East Anglia. Intensively cultivated, they yield a large proportion of the nation's fresh vegetable supplies.

A little distance downstream the River Great Ouse is joined by Soham Lode, the only one of the Cambridgeshire Lodes to flow into the Great Ouse, the other Lodes joining the River Cam, 5km to the south at Upware. Derived from the medieval word meaning waterway, the Lodes form a unique network of waterways which link the main river with villages lying on the edge of the chalk uplands to the east. Whilst some say they were built as boundary markers or as a series of defences across the fens, they are more generally considered to have been built by the Romans as transport canals. Their heyday was between the 17th and 19th centuries and lasted until the advent of the railways in 1884.

When they were first built there was no fen drainage and they would have passed through swampy lands. As the fens were drained, the soil shrank, the land level dropped and the Lodes became high level carriers across the fens. During the 1970s, due to the increasing cost of maintaining their integrity, there was much controversy concerning their future. This centred around either retaining the existing high level system with its attendant costs of maintaining watercourses which did not leak into the lower Fenland, or building a new low lying network of drains to convey both upland water and drainage water across the fens. In this later proposal, the Lodes would have been retained, but as redundant watercourses. In the event, the original high level system was adopted and the Lodes are now preserved in embanked channels running across the fen.

Soham Lode is the longest of the Cambridgeshire Lodes. It skirts the edge of the former Soham Mere where, according to a medieval tradition, a boat race was held between monks from Ely and Ramsey for the bones of St Felix. He had been installed by Honorius, fifth Archbishop of Canterbury, as the first Bishop of East Anglia, and, in 631 founded a monastery in Soham, where, in about 647, he was buried. Some 400 years later his remains were removed from Ely's jurisdiction to that of Ramsey Abbey. Hence this rivalry between these two great ecclesiastical houses.

The Ely to Ipswich railway line runs beside the Lode as it skirts the old Mere. On 2 June 1944 at Soham railway station, the driver of a 51 wagon train of ammunition, Ben Gimbert, realised that the first wagon was on fire. He and his fireman James Nightall uncoupled it from the rest of the train and tried to pull it through the station into open country. It blew up about 100m away from the main train, killed Nightall and the signal man, severely injured Gimbert, destroyed the station and damaged houses up to 1km away. But for the heroic actions of Gimbert and Nightall, the whole town would have been devastated. As it was, 761 buildings were damaged; thirteen beyond repair.

Between Pope's Corner and Ely, the fen is at its narrowest and it was the obvious place for causeways, ferries and bridges between the Isle and the "mainland". There is evidence of a late Bronze Age pile and faggot causeway leading from New Fordey Farm at Barway to the Ouse River opposite Little Thetford, whose early names Thiutford (c972) and Liteltedford (c1086) both imply a major river crossing. The most likely spot for William the Conqueror to launch his attack on Hereward the Wake and where the Battle of *Alrehed* took place, is a little further downstream, between Stuntney and Braham Farm. To support this theory, there were reasonable foundations for a short causeway whose length was consistent with contemporary accounts, there are remains of a medieval camp near Braham Farm, Braham itself was of some importance, as it features in early 17th century maps as Breame or Brame; in the early 14th century nearby land was called "Herewardsbech", a local stream was called The Alderbrook, an area of land between Witchford and Ely is know today as Alderforth and, most significantly, a number of 11th century weapons have been recovered from the river.

The last known causeway to cross the River Ouse to the Isle did so just upstream from Ely and again dates from the Bronze Age. At the time of its building, the river flowed north east from near the present railway bridge to pass close under Stuntney before turning north towards Prickwillow and Littleport. According to legend, the causeway's route from Soham and Stuntney to Ely was disclosed in a dream to St Edmund, King of the East Angles. Not only did it enable monks to travel between St Felix' monastery in Soham and St Etheldreda's monastery in Ely, but it was to become an important Roman Road connecting Ely via Soham with Colchester, one of the four *colonia* or local administration centres in Roman Britain.

Whilst the ancient course of the River Ouse was to well to the east, its present continues north towards Ely following a former watercourse which opened up into a large expanse of water that would have lapped the edge of the highest part of the Isle and upon which Ely was to be established.

Of all the Marshland Isles, I Ely am the Queene

Ely, Saxon Elig or Latin Elge, meaning Eel Island, stands high above the surrounding drained fenland dominating with its great cathedral, "The Ship of the Fens", some of the richest agricultural land in the country. To see the Isle crowned by the cathedral rising above an early morning mist or against the background of a summer thunderstorm must rank as one of the most unforgettable views in the Country.

In 673 St Æthelthryth (St Etheldreda or St Audry) founded her monastery at Ely. She was born at Exning in c630, the daughter of Anna King of the East Angles. Little more than a child herself, she married the 14 year old Prince Tonbert. He died some three years later and she vowed to remain a virgin. For 'political' reasons she married Prince Egfrid (Ecgfrith), another boy prince. As he grew up, not unnaturally he wanted to consummate his marriage but Etheldreda remained true to her vows. Egfrid approached Bishop Wilfrid of York seeking his help to release Etheldreda from her vows. The Bishop refused and actually helped Etheldreda to escape her husband's clutches. Once free of him, she entered the religious life as abbess of her monastery at Ely. Bede tells that after her death in 679, either from the plague or as a consequence of a very large goitre, her body, which was found to be incorrupt and without the large goitre, was disinterred by her sister and successor, Abbess Seaxburh (St Sexburga) and reburied in a white marble coffin in Ely. She was wont to say, "I know I deservedly bear the weight of sickness on my neck, for I remember, when I was very young, I bore there the needless weight of jewels."

Many spiritual powers have been attributed to her. According to a legend, during Henry I's reign, there was a man called Brytstan, who lived near Ely at Chatteris and who made his living by usury. He fell very sick and vowed that if he recovered he would become a monk in Etheldreda's monastery. He recovered but whilst he was preparing to honour his vow, he was visited by Robert Malarte, a servant to both the King and the Devil, who accused him of falsely wishing to become a monk in order to conceal his previous wrong doings. Although innocent, he was tried in Huntingdon and condemned by false witness. He was imprisoned in London where he was tortured and where he remained in chains for months. During this time he prayed ceaselessly to St Benedict and St Etheldreda, to whose services he had already vowed himself. One night he awoke, aware of two figures one of which said she was Etheldreda and the other was Benedict "in whose habit Brytstan wished to become a servant of God". Benedict took two links of the chains and simply drew them apart. He then discarded the chains with such force that he woke the guards. On seeing the prisoner had been released, the matter was reported to Queen Matilda, one of whose chaplains declared that a miracle had occurred. Whilst the Queen wanted to keep the iron collar and chains, she allowed Brytstan to take them with him back to the monastery. Returning with all honour to Ely, now a monk, he placed the chains before the altar. For years pilgrims to St Etheldreda's shrine were given small shackles like the originals. As time went on these "St Awdry's Chains" degenerated into plaited ribbons which could be bought at local fairs, and a custom evolved for English women to wear a very light chain necklace made of fine silk; Etheldreda's Chain.

Her monastery flourished until it was sacked by the Danes in 869. A hundred years was to pass before it was re-organised as a convent of Benedictine monks. As a result of many gifts of land, it soon became very wealthy and in 1082 Abbot Simeon started the building of the present cathedral. Again the great monastery flourished until the Dissolution of the Monasteries in 1539 when it was reorganised, mercifully, as Dean and Chapter. Unfortunately Oliver Cromwell, in spite of being Steward of the Ely Tithes, Governor of the Isle of Ely, Champion of the Rights of Fenmen and living in the city, was not so merciful; not only did he decapitate all but one of the delicate statues in the Lady Chapel, but in January 1644, he dismissed the congregation, drove them out, and closed the cathedral for the next 17 years.

The cathedral is surrounded by buildings connected with it, the early monastery and latterly the King's School. Some of the monastic buildings include a part of the 12th century Monk's Infirmary, the timber-framed 14th century Powchers Hall, the blood-letting house of the early monastery where monks were bled by leeches to keep their bodies "in balance", a 13th century Black Hostelry, accommodation for black robed monks from other Benedictine monasteries and the 14th century Porta, the main entrance to the monastery and once used as the prior's prison.

In 1321, John of Crauden was appointed Prior, and in 1330 he built the small Prior Crauden's Chapel and the Queen's Hall, possibly to entertain his special friend Queen Phillipa, wife of Edward III. When she visited Ely she gave her jewelled robes of state which she had worn in thanksgiving after the birth of the Black Prince and from which the prior made three copes.

The Palace Green leads past the 15th century Bishop's Palace built by John Alcock. Not only had he been Bishop of Rochester, Worcester, Ely and Lincoln, but he went on to become Lord Chancellor and in 1479 founded St John's College, Cambridge. In contrast to the palace, the cathedral and to the parish church of St Mary, which probably stands on the site of the first religious settlement on the Isle founded in 597 by St Augustine, is a large cannon given to the city after its capture from the Russians at Sebastopol. It is aimed almost directly at the thirteenth century half timbered and reputedly haunted Cromwell House, formerly the rectory and parsonage of Holy Trinity and St Mary's and latterly, for ten years, the home of the Lord Protector!

Just to the north of Ely, the River Great Ouse flows past the small settlement of Queen Adelaide in memory of a local pub named after the unpopular queen of King William IV. There is an ancient tale of a beautiful shepherd's wife who kept bees here and who was much coveted by the monks at Ely. Accordingly a knight agreed to kidnap her. When he arrived at her home, she hid and watched him enter the house where he helped himself to some mead, some of which splashed down his breast-plate. Eventually he found the woman and dragged her from her hiding. She shouted for help but none was forthcoming so she called for her bees. They responded immediately and swarms attacked the knight. Encouraged by the spilt mead they soon crawled all over him, stinging him under his armour. To escape he jumped into the river and, because of the weight of his armour, was immediately drowned. Bees were still kept at a small house at Queen Adelaide in the late 1990s.

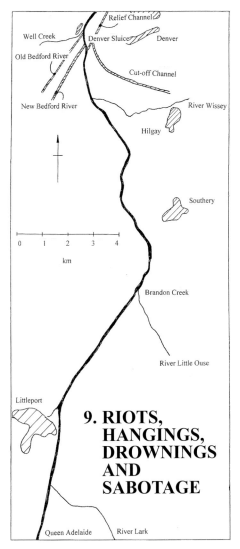

The map shows the region with the following labels:
Relief Channel, Well Creek, Denver Sluice, Denver, Old Bedford River, Cut-off Channel, New Bedford River, River Wissey, Hilgay, Southery, Brandon Creek, River Little Ouse, Littleport, Queen Adelaide, River Lark

0   1   2   3   4
km

9. RIOTS, HANGINGS, DROWNINGS AND SABOTAGE

The Adelaide Course, a monotonous, long, straight, man-made stretch, variously known as the Ely Ouse, or the Ten Mile River, and which the Cambridge University boat race crews use for training, is joined by the River Lark and leads to Littleport. Standing on its own small Fenland isle, close to ancient rivers, Littleport is somewhat of an enigma with few buildings of any great antiquity. There can be little doubt that it has always been over shadowed by Ely. It is in a lonely part of the country, described not so long ago as "the loneliest spot within 100 miles of London" whilst of the town itself it was said in the 1750s that it was as "rare to see a coach in Littleport as a ship in Newmarket". Poverty, exploitation and starvation undoubtedly occasioned the Littleport Riots of May 1816.

(See colour section for larger photo)

Faced with unemployment, near starvation, high prices, and having no voting powers nor Trades Unions, farm labourers and soldiers returning from the Napoleonic Wars, provoked by a local farmer who owned much of the nearby farm land, Henry Martin finally rebelled. Summoned by a horn usually used by lightermen, the rioters gathered at the Globe Public House and waited for more followers from Southery and Denver to arrive, before marching to the vicarage, the vicar also being the local magistrate. Offered little, and somewhat the worse for drink, they attacked a number of houses and the vicarage. The vicar read the Riot Act and tried to defend his home, but in the end had to flee with his family to Ely to seek help.

Meanwhile some of the rioters decided to march on Ely, armed with farm implements, pistols and a wagon carrying large fenland punt guns. After a meeting outside the White Hart in Ely, magistrates agreed to the rioters' demands for work and food, and after some debate, agreed to pardon them all. Whilst many returned to Littleport, some went on a celebratory, drunken spree in Ely breaking in to shops and houses. An Ely lawyer, Thomas Archer rode to Bury St Edmunds to seek assistance from the militia and the magistrates appealed to the Home Secretary for help. Sixteen dragoons arrived and a prebendary magistrate, Sir Henry Bate Dudley, nicknamed 'The Fighting Parson' and aged 71, led the dragoons and yeomanry at a gallop back to Littleport.

On 24 May 1816 a pitched battle took place at the George Public House. Over two days, a trooper and several rioters were wounded, one rioter was killed and there were 98 arrests. A Commission was set up to try 76 prisoners. The Justice was Edward Christian, chief justice of the Isle of Ely and a professor of law at Cambridge, also brother of Fletcher Christian of HMS Bounty. On 22 June, 24 rioters were sentenced to death. In the event five were executed in Ely on 28 June, the remainder being deported. Their memorial is in St Mary's Church, Ely. As one rioter had remarked earlier: "I might as well be hanged as starved".

Still in a man made channel, now constrained between massive flood banks, the river continues to flow north above and across a monotonous low lying agricultural landscape punctuated by straight lines of drains, rivers, roads, railways, and electricity cables. It can be a hard country possessed of a unique beauty. In dry weather the almost ever present winds can whip up the soil and seeds into great black clouds which sweep across the tree-less lands like a sandstorm, known locally as a 'Fen Blow'. In wet weather the drainage ditches run bank full and pumps struggle to keep the waters from flooding onto the surrounding land by pumping into an already brim full River Ouse. Winters can be bitterly cold when dykes and sluice gates freeze; summers can be roasting hot when thunderstorms sweep across the vast skyscape. Those who can overcome the rigours of these fens, love them.

The Ouse is joined by the River Little Ouse at Brandon Creek, where it leaves Cambridgeshire and enters Norfolk. Despite the somewhat regulated aspect of the countryside, there is a certain mysterious atmosphere. Who lived at Priests Houses, a riverside settlement shown on early 17th century maps? What is the truth that lies behind the legends surrounding the Inn at Brandon Creek? Reputedly first built by Dutch engineers in about 1640 who had employed prisoners of war to dig their drainage works, tales are told of violent and macabre killings along the banks of a river which, at that time, was tidal. Some, when the tide was out, were buried up to their necks in the muddy river banks where they were left to drown as the tide slowly rose. Others, when the tide was in, were made to stand on barges with a noose, attached to overhanging trees, around their necks. As the tide dropped they were slowly strangled. On a quiet misty evening it is all too easy to imagine their ghosts.

The road bridge at Ten Mile bank leads to Hilgay just to the east on the River Wissey. It was here in the Elizabethan Wood Hall once a grange of the abbots of Ramsey, that George William Manby, who had been born nearby at Denver in 1765, made his home. Although a member of the Cambridgeshire militia, he had strong links with the sea; he was a schoolfellow of Nelson, and his brother Thomas was a Rear Admiral. After hopelessly witnessing ships in distress and unable to help, he invented in 1808 at Hilgay, an apparatus for firing a line from a mortar to a ship. It is said that he carried out his experiments from the tower of Hilgay parish church, situated at the end of a beautiful avenue of 60 lime trees interspersed with holly bushes, and of which he was a churchwarden! Within 15 years, use of the mortar had resulted in some 230 lives being saved. For this he was awarded a sum of £2,000 by parliament and made a Fellow of the Royal Society in 1831.

So, after a rather featureless stretch of river, where people say that "it is quite exciting to see a cow on the banks", or "this is the best place to complete your income tax returns", the river flows on towards Denver Sluice. Brooding over the landscape, it is one of the finest combined flood defence, land drainage, water resources and navigation structures and complexes in the United Kingdom. It is here that waters which started their journey in Buckinghamshire, Bedfordshire, Northamptonshire, Cambridgeshire, Essex, Suffolk, and Norfolk all come together.

The first structure at Denver had been built by Vermuyden in about 1652. He had "thought it necessary to shutt out the tydes from cominge the old way up to Harrimeer [i.e. up the Ouse to near Ely] by a dam made over the Old Ouze near Salter's Lode". Others also thought it would similarly prevent waters from Bedford and beyond that had passed down the New Bedford River from Earith to Denver from flowing back to Ely. Despite petitions from the town and University of Cambridge, he built a dam with a 7.25m wide lock, "with fresh water doors thereby to bee able both to hold in and lett goe the water, as there should bee occasion, and preserve the navigation from Cambridge".

Within 10 years, however, there were problems which continue today. Whilst Vermuyden understood that he could hasten the evacuation of water, particularly in times of flood, by cutting straight embanked channels, he may not have fully appreciated that he also needed a sufficient gradient to speed the flow. Even if he had appreciated this, there would have been nothing he could have done about it. Whilst the water level at the sluice is between one or two meters above sea level, it is 25.7km from the sea, at King's Lynn. Two further complications had arisen, because first the bed of the New Bedford River was a little higher than the bed of the Great Ouse, and secondly the flood tides were (and still are) much stronger than the ebb tides. There were a number of consequences. The flood tides brought sand and silt up the river from the Wash which was then deposited below the sluice and at the outfall of the New Bedford River. The ebb tides and the summer flow were of insufficient strength to scour these silts which consequently accumulated. Not only could the navigation gates be opened to provide some limited scour, but whilst the winter flows came down the New Bedford

River in great volumes they still had insufficient force to scour away the silts. This resulted in both problems for navigation and, ironically, upstream flooding. It was an "ill formed, and still worse executed Project". Despite some unsuccessful modifications made in 1682, many petitions and sabotage attempts to blow it up, the sluice remained in operation until 1713, when it collapsed because of the combined pressures caused by the combination of a fluvial flood and a flood tide.

Those that had opposed the sluice now expected benefits, but they were not forthcoming. The collapse had left obstructions for navigation, flood waters did indeed flow up towards Ely and the condition of the river deteriorated. After much conflicting debate, the sluice was rebuilt between 1748 and 1750 under the direction of Charles Labelye, a Swiss engineer. The new sluice performed little better than its predecessor and in 1751 Nathaniel Kinderley proposed, as a solution, that the meandering natural course of the river to King's Lynn be shortened by nearly 10km through the construction of a straight new cut, the Eau Brink Cut. Due to further opposition, wars and rising costs, the cut was not completed until 1821, shortly after which, in 1832, Denver Sluice was totally rebuilt to a design by Sir John Rennie. Still the arguments continued and even this new sluice was said to be useless for both flood protection and navigation; it should be demolished. Even all the works of the 1960s, described earlier, and further refurbishment whilst providing an improvement in flood protection, have largely failed to stop the problems of siltation.

However, they were to provide an unforeseen benefit to water resources. In the early 1970s modifications were made which enabled water from the Great Ouse to be diverted into the Cut-off Channel from whence it was abstracted near Hockwold and fed via a series of pumps, pipes, tunnels and natural and artificial rivers to reservoirs some 145km distant in Essex. It was one of the first examples of a "water grid" within which water from Buckinghamshire, Northamptonshire, Bedfordshire, Cambridgeshire and Norfolk was used to supply South Essex.

To ease the problems for navigators, a new lock was built at Denver in 2000 enabling vessels to proceed to King's Lynn via the non tidal Relief Channel. A new lock at the Tail Sluice of this Channel would then enable vessels to re-enter the tidal Great Ouse (the Eau Brink Cut) just south of King's Lynn and a few kilometres from the sea.

As well as being the birthplace of George Manby, who is commemorated as "Fellow of the Royal Society, Inventor and Sailor", Denver was the home of Robert Brady, historian, physician to Charles II and James II, and Master of Caius College, Cambridge and of the Willoughbys who in the early 17th century owned much fenland to the north of the river and whose family seat was the Tudor Denver Hall.

Before leaving the non-tidal waters for good, a sluice and a lock, half a kilometre below Denver Sluice, give access to the Middle Level, a vast area of Fenland lying between Denver and Peterborough, and Earith and Wisbech. Both formed an integral part of Vermuyden's drainage works. When he built the Old Bedford River from Earith, he needed to prevent the tidal water from flowing back up the Old Bedford River, so he built a stone sluice "of great strength" at the out-fall of the Old Bedford River into the tidal River Ouse. Similarly, he needed another sluice to keep the water out of the Middle Level itself and so a "great sasse" (lock) was built on the ancient Welle Creek at Salter's Lode. There is still, in the true sense, a sluice on the Old Bedford River, navigable only when the water levels are equal on either side. The "great sasse" at Salter's Lode was replaced with a lock in 1827 which provides the main access to a unique network of old rivers and fenland drains, many of which are navigable and enable a through passage to the River Nene at Peterborough.

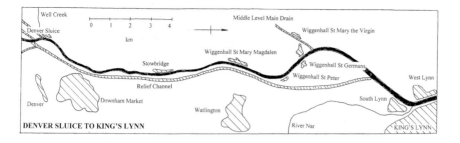

The Roman east west Fen Causeway, which had crossed the river just upstream from Denver Sluice, was diverted to pass through the early town of Downham Market. Although of no great size it started life as Downham Hythe, a small, but significant inland river port. The market was established in 1050 by the monks of Ramsey Abbey and gradually the town moved away from the river towards the church and the King's Lynn to Ely road, only to move back again towards the river with the coming of the railway in 1846/7. Whilst full support was given to the Littleport rioters in 1816, the town, with its miniature cast iron Big Ben clock, built in 1878 by William Cunliffe at a cost of £450, belies two important personages. In the spring of 1646, Charles I, travelling between Oxford and King's Lynn and hoping either to escape or to gain support, is said to have stayed here disguised as a clergyman. On the same journey he is also said to have stayed at the nearby mid 15th century Snowre or Snore Hall, hiding in a 3m by 6m secret chamber. Despite the disguise and the hiding places, he was unsuccessful in his mission and later gave himself up in Newark. In complete contrast, Horatio Nelson attended the small local school with his friend George Manby.

The small settlement of Stowbridge belies its past even more than Downham Market. At the end of the 12th century there was "no habitation nor ground yielding profit", except for Crabhouse Abbey for Augustinian nuns. To protect what little land there was and to enable more marshy land to be recovered, the Old Podyke was raised in 1223. Running between Stowbridge and Outwell, it protected the land from the upland waters. In 1259 the first Commission of Sewers was established. The Commissioners became the conservators of the Fens and it was they who set out the fundamental principals of payment for flood protection and land drainage works which have been followed religiously into the 21st century. These principals were that every landowner should contribute financially to the works in proportion to the area of land protected and the benefits received. In the case of the Old Podyke, every acre of land was deemed to be responsible for one foot of the dyke. Despite these arrangements, by 1422 the Commissioners decided that, mainly because of weak foundations, the bank was incapable of further repair. It was abandoned and a the New

Podyke was built further south between Outwell and Salter's Lode.

During the Middle Ages. the silt fens to the east of the river were drained, agricultural activity increased and, combined with the growth of King's Lynn as a port, these fens became one of the most prosperous areas of Norfolk. With all this new found prosperity, single parishes grew and often divided. One such parish was Wiggenhall, which by the end of the 14th century had divided into four separate parishes each with its own magnificent church, another pointer to the wealth of the region. Proceeding down stream, the River Great Ouse passes through these four parishes.

Wiggenhall St Mary Magdalen lies on the west bank. Its church, whilst somewhat decayed, is notable for some medieval glasswork, believed to be the gift of Isabel of Ingoldsthorpe in 1470, showing a number of uncommon saints, such as St Callistus, St Britius and St Romanus. The former East Anglian Railway Company line from King's Lynn to March via Wisbech passed through this Wiggenhall; its station name, Magdalen Road, being clipped out of a box hedge.

Next on the east bank is Wiggenhall St Peter, its once magnificent church now a striking roofless ruin. A little further downstream and the river flows between Wiggenhall St Mary The Virgin to the west and Wiggenhall St Germans to the east. St Mary The Virgin is in the country on the way to St Mary's Hall, dating in part from around 1500, once the home of the 16th century Kervill family and now much altered following "restoration" during the Victorian period. The church, maintained by the Redundant Churches

Fund, is known for its albeit restored but almost complete set of 16th century benches showing Saints and other motifs. These however almost pale into insignificance when compared with the benches at St Germans. Here there is a remarkable collection of dark, almost perfect, 15th century benches, on the ends of which are carved Saints, groups of people, lovers, drunkards, a priest blessing a kneeling person and grotesques.

Two more pieces of the jigsaw that makes up the story of the drainage of this region are to be found just downstream from Wiggenhall St Mary the Virgin and Wiggenhall St Germans. In the mid 18th century the river flowed from St Germans in a long westerly loop. In 1751, Nathaniel Kinderley revived his father's idea of a new cut to eliminate this 9.5km detour and consequently improve the gradient and thus help to scour the river of shoals. After years of discussion, the Eau Brink Act was passed in 1795 enabling the raising of finance. However, because of further disputes, the Napoleonic War and escalating costs, the works were not actually completed until July 1821. The consequences were immediately beneficial, but not as great as had been hoped.

The final phase to effectively drain the Middle Level took place almost immediately afterwards in 1844, when a Bill was passed enabling rates to be levied for the building of the Middle Level Main drain running directly from Popham's Eau south of Upwell to join the Ouse via a new sluice at Wiggenhall St Germans. Once again there was much fierce opposition based on the belief that flood waters with the attendant risk of flooding, were simply being shifted from place to place. The works were eventually completed in 1848. It was not long before some of the opposition's fears were realised. On 4 may 1862, the sluice "blew up". Not only did immediate serious flooding result, but the tide went up the new drain which consequently breached and 6,000 acres were flooded. After some temporary measures, a new sluice was installed in 1880. However, this too began to fail; as the fens were drained, so they sank and the gravity outfall of the sluice ceased. A combined pumping station, initially with three diesel pumps, and sluice were installed in 1934. A fourth pump was added in 1951 and the whole station converted to electricity in 1970.

Charles I was not the only King to cross the river nearby. In October 1216, King John left King's Lynn for Newark where he died, via Wisbech, which at that time was right on the edge of the coast. The King's route took him across the river, which at that date was only a relatively small river, near Wiggenhall St Germans. He crossed to Wiggenhall St Mary the Virgin and continued on relatively high ground to Tilney and Wisbech. Whilst it is most likely that he "lost his treasure" near Wisbech, land over which he might have passed always fetched a higher price than other surrounding land. Was he poisoned and thus lost track of his treasure? The speculation as to the treasure's whereabouts will continue.

> *I am known as the bad King John,*
> *The English Throne I sat upon;*
> *I sit on every one in sight,*
> *For sitting on things was my delight.*
> *I signed the Magna Charta, too,*
> *The earliest form of I.O.U.*
> *In the Wash I lost my lingerie,*
> *and gained a name in historie.*

So the river reaches King's Lynn, dating from Saxon times, and whose name originates from "llyn" or "lin", a small lake, in this instance lying in the flood plain of the rivers Great Ouse and the Nar. Whilst the earliest settlement was probably at South Lynn, another settlement became established a little to the north around a small Benedictine priory established in c1100 by the first Bishop of Norwich, Bishop Herbert de Losinga who had been an abbot at Ramsey before moving to Norwich via Thetford. Land was given to the monks and a market and fair were granted. St Margaret's white limestone church, dating from the middle of the 12th century, now stands on the site of the priory and the Saturday Market continues. Inside the church are two of the biggest and most famous brasses in England. Both probably Flemish, they depict Adam de Walsokne and his wife (1349) with windmills and horsemen at their feet and Robert Braunche (1364) with his wife (wives?) and mourners.

The next land to be settled, just to the north of Purfleet, was developed between 1150 and 1170 by the next Bishop of Norwich, Bishop William Turbus and had its own chapel of St Nicholas, fair, and market, the Tuesday Market. During the 13th century, the Bishop bought back the land that had been given to the monks and a town, Bishop's Lynn, developed as a single entity, its first charter having been received from King John in 1204.

The town remained under the jurisdiction of the Bishops of Norwich until the reign of Henry VIII. Not un-naturally there were other religious developments. St James' Chapel was built in the early 1100s. Later converted into a workhouse, it's site is at the Methodist St James' Chapel (1858). Greyfriars, one of many Friar's Houses with its octagonal tower dating from the late 14th century, was founded c1230-5. Red Mount Chapel, is one of the most strangest Gothic churches in England. In plan, a cross within a brick octagon, it dates from 1485 and was a wayside chapel, built on an artificial mound, for pilgrims making their way east to Walsingham.

In contrast to the growth of religious foundations, the town developed rapidly during the Middle Ages towards the river and its "fleets", tidal channels which acted as simple docks, to become one of the biggest commercial ports in England, at one time second only to London. During King John's reign the port dues were 2/3rds that of London and when Edward III sent an expedition to France, 19 ships sailed from Lynn compared with 24 from London. The basis of the trade, wool, cloth, timber, coal and grain, was trans-shipment of goods from the Hanseatic ports in Germany, Sweden and Norway from ocean going vessels into warehouses and thence to smaller vessels and barges for passage inland along the River Ouse and its tributaries. There were 30 Guilds, of which the Guild of the Holy Trinity was the largest and virtually ran the town by itself, and its chequered flint and stone Guildhall built in 1421 survives. Amongst Lynn's regalia are the beautiful silver and enamel King John Cup, (the earliest medieval secular cup in England, but probably not English and actually dating from the mid 14th century), the medieval King John Sword (also probably dating from the mid 14th century) and the Red Register, a record of commercial transactions and one of the oldest paper books in existence, the first record being made in 1307.

After the growth in the Middle Ages, the Bishops transferred their lands to Henry VIII. Henceforth the town became known as Lynn Regis or King's Lynn. The port continued to thrive and a Merchants Exchange was built near the Quay in 1683; later it was to become the Customs House.

Amongst the infamous of King's Lynn are Eugene Aram and Joseph Beeton. Eugene Aram, an usher at Knaresborough school, with an accomplice, murdered one Daniel Clarke in 1745 after becoming suspicious of his wife's conduct with Daniel. After the murder, he moved to King's Lynn where he became an assistant at the grammar school. Some 13 years later he was betrayed by his accomplice, traced to King's Lynn, taken to York, tried and executed.

> *Two stern faced men set out from Lynn,*
> *Through the cold and heavy mist,*
> *And Eugene Aram walked between,*
> *With gyves upon his wrist.*

In the 18th century, hanging often resulted in the slow strangulation of the condemned. Those of spirit would fling themselves out to avoid such agonies and one to do so was Joseph Beeton, 20, who was executed in 1783 in front of 5,000 spectators, on the Saddlebow Road near the South Gate. His crime was robbery of the mail coach but it was also said that he had been a martyr to the villainy of a friend.

In contrast, the most famous names associated with King's Lynn reflect its erstwhile importance as a great sea port.

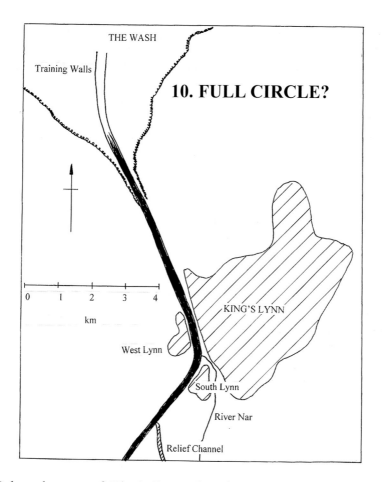

THE WASH

Training Walls

10. FULL CIRCLE?

0 1 2 3 4

km

KING'S LYNN

West Lynn

South Lynn

River Nar

Relief Channel

Below the port of King's Lynn, the River Great Ouse, now free of encumbrances, is on the final stage of its 260km journey to the Wash and the open sea. Those who have sailed down this last stretch of river include Friar Nicholas of Lynn (d1369) who voyaged to Iceland and is the reputed discoverer of the Americas; King Edward IV who fled to Flanders from Lynn in 1460; Captain John Smith (1580-1631), a Virginia Pioneer who founded New England and who was allegedly rescued from the Indians by the Indian Princess Pocahontas; Admiral James Burney (1750-1821) an explorer (whose father was Dr Charles Burney, author, musician and organist at St Margaret's Church and whose sister Francis d'Arbilay (nee Fanny Burney), the famous novelist was born in King's Lynn in 1752); Captain George Vancouver (1757-1798), who searched for the North west Passage and acquired British Columbia for the crown; Admiral Lord Nelson (1758-1805); the Arctic explorer Admiral Sir Edward Parry (1799-1855); and Captain Samuel Gurney Cresswell (1827-1867), the first man to navigate the north west passage.

There are plans to join the upper reaches of the Great Ouse with the Grand Union Canal and hence to the Thames. There are also proposals to extend the non tidal navigation from Denver, the last few kilometres to the tidal quays of the Port of Kings Lynn, via a new short canal leading to the once navigable River Nar. At an estimated cost of £6.5m (2001), it would open up for the adventurous navigator a wealth of circular routes through the Wash to the Rivers Nene and Thames.

Although the river has now reached the end of its journey, it is not the end of the story, but simply the end of one segment of a circle. One simply has to look at the flood markers at the entrance to St Margaret's Church and the wooden groves to accommodate flood boards at the front doors of many houses to appreciate the threat posed by the sea.

The sea, in dense darkness began to be agitated by the violence of the wind and burst through its accustomed limits, occupying town, fields and inundating parts which no age in past times had been recorded to have been covered with sea water, for issuing forth in the middle of the night it suffocated or drowned men and women sleeping in their beds with infants in their cradles and many kinds of cattle. Many when surrounded by the waters sought a place of refuge by mounting into trees but benumbed by the cold, they fell in and were drowned.

John of Oxnead, December 1247.

Long before mankind intervened, the river naturally carved out its own channel and flood plain in the upper reaches. The flood plain was an essential and integral part of the river system. Whenever the river was in flood and its channel could not accommodate the flood waters, it spread, without a problem, onto the surrounding flood plains. Its passage to the newly formed Fenland was unimpeded. Once in the Fens it found its way to the sea through a myriad of lakes, lagoons, channels and streams. The frequent floods were of no consequence to this unworked and uninhabited land. Throughout its length it achieved a measure of balance with nature which was to be upset by mankind.

In the upper reaches, settlements became established near the river. They grew into villages and towns; some began to encroach onto the natural flood plain. Unsurprisingly, from time to time, they were flooded. The same villages and towns encouraged trade; mills were built by the river, road crossings were needed and navigation started. Obstructions, which helped some and hindered others, appeared on the river. As the years went by there was more building in the flood plain which again, not surprisingly, was subject to flooding. The risk of that flooding became higher as the space in the flood plains was gradually taken up by the developments. Development was not of course confined to the flood plain and further developments throughout the catchment, with their large built up and paved areas, dramatically altered the pattern of run-off to the river. Change was not confined to the river valley. On the higher lands which fed the river, the agricultural industry was growing. The characteristics of the natural upland run-off was altered not only by the crops themselves but also, very significantly, by improvements in soil drainage.

Thus, as a direct consequence of man's own actions, the natural characteristics of the river were gradually changed, more water was fed into the river faster than before, flood protection schemes were required and it was no longer free to run its own course.

Mankind was to create further problems for itself in the river's lower reaches and in Fenland. The direct consequence of draining the fens was that they shrank. As they shrank, not only because of the drainage, but also because of soil wastage through the intense agricultural activities, natural gravity outfalls disappeared, and pumps had to be installed. The rivers' embankments had to be increased in breadth and height, to cope with not only the pumped Fenland water, but also the increased volumes of water from the upland catchment.

All in all, the River Great Ouse is now constrained and restrained. Despite the efforts to keep it so there are occasions when it breaks out, sometimes with catastrophic and fatal consequences. A direct fight against nature has little chance of success. On the other hand, a partnership with nature, combined with proper planning and development controls, is much more likely to succeed.

Two other mechanisms, one natural and one man made, are having possibly an even greater effect on the river. The first is a legacy of the Ice Age; East Anglia is slowly sinking. The second is a consequence of the "Greenhouse Effect"; the sea level is slowly rising. These two mechanisms combine and the river, with its increased volumes of water, finds that the gradient of its final run to the sea is decreasing. Even this is not the end of the story as the "Greenhouse Effect" is causing one other crucial climate change; the frequency and intensity of storms is increasing.

So at the start of the 21st century, the River Great Ouse finds itself having to cope more frequently with larger, faster volumes of water, which it then has to discharge to the sea, which itself is influenced by more frequent storm surge tides, through a channel whose gradient is generally decreasing and in which silts are being deposited.

Throughout history there have been disastrous fluvial and tidal floods. They will continue and it is all too easy to see how within a relatively short span of geological time, the Fens, as indeed forecast by the Board of Agriculture in 1925, could "return to primeval conditions". All it could take to precipitate the start of this return would be a combination of two principal events which have already occurred, albeit mercifully separately. First would be a fluvial flood, perhaps triggered by a rapid thaw of thick snow, accompanied by heavy rain, similar to the 1947 floods. The second would be a tidal flood resulting from a tidal surge on an already high spring tide, similar to the 1953 flood in which so many people were drowned in both England and Holland or the even higher 1978 surge tide. However sophisticated the weather forecasting and flood warning systems are, should such combinations of floods of such magnitude occur and the flood defences fail, then the consequences would be catastrophic.

In no branch of engineering, perhaps, is there so little unanimity of opinion, or in which so much money is from time to time expended on works which are useless.   *W. H. Wheeler 1902.*

REFERENCES AND FURTHER READING

The Author gratefully acknowledges the authors of the following publications and maps which have been used extensively whilst researching the background to this book.

A Dictionary of English Place Names, A. D. Mills, Oxford, 1991.

A Geology for Engineers, F. G. H. Blyth, Arnold, 1961.

A Haunting Beauty, E. Thompson, Sunday Telegraph, 2000,

A History of Huntingdonshire, M. Wickes, Oxford, 1985.

A House Frozen in Childhood, M. Thompson, Sunday Telegraph, 1996.

A Short History of Ely Cathedral, S. Evans, Camb. Univ. Press, 1946.

A View into Cambridgeshire, M. Rouse, Dalton, 1974.

An Atlas of Cambridgeshire and Huntingdonshire History,
    ed. T. Kirby and S. Oostuizen, Anglia Polytechnic University, 2000.

Anglo Saxon England, P. Hunter Blair, Camb.Univ.Press. 1956.

Bedfordshire, L. Meynell, Hale, 1950.

Bedfordshire and Huntingdonshire Landscape, P. Bigmore,
    Hodder and Stoughton, 1979.

Bedfordshire and Huntingdonshire, A. Mee, Hodder and Stoughton,
    1973.

Buckinghamshire, A. Mee, Hodder and Stoughton, 1965.

Buckinghamshire, B. Watkin, Faber, 1981.

Buckinghamshire, E. S. Roscoe, Methuen, 1903.

Cambridgeshire, A. Mee, Hodder and Stoughton, 1939.

Cambridgeshire, N. Scarfe, Faber & Faber, 1983.

Cambridgeshire Customs and Folklore, E. Porter, Routledge, Kegan
    Paul, 1969.

Curiosities of Rural Cambridgeshire, P. Jeever, Oleander Press, 1977.

Daily Telegraph, J. Rozenberg, 18 October, 2000.

East Anglia, R. H. Mottram, Chapman and Hall, 1933.

East Anglia, H. Innes, Hodder and Stoughton, 1990.

East Anglia, D. Wallace, Batsford, 1939.

Ely Cathedral, C. W. Stubbs, Dent, 1879.

Ely Town Trail and Mini Guide to Ely, East Cambs. Dist. Council,
    1999.

England's Thousand Best Churches, S. Jenkins, Penguin, 1999.

Fenland; Its Ancient Past and Uncertain Future, H. Godwin, Camb.
    Univ. Press, 1978.

Fenland River, R. Tibbs, Dalton, 1969.

Fenland Rivers, I. Wedgewood, Rich and Cowan, 1936.

Fenland Waterways, M. Roulstone, Balfour, 1974.

Forgotten Railways of East Anglia, R. S. Joby, David and Charles, 1977.

Geology and Scenery in England and Wales. A. E. Trueman, Pelican, 1963.

Ghosts and Legends of Lincolnshire and the Fen Country, P. Howat, Countryside Books, 1992.

Godmanchester, H. J. M. Green, Oleander Press, 1977.

Hemingford Abbots, C. R. Beresford and R. B. Butterfield, Hemingford Abbots PLC, 1995.

Hemingford Grey, M. Carter, Westmeare Publications, 1998.

Historical Memorials of Ely Cathedral. C. W. Stubbs, Dent, 1897.

History of Bluntisham cum Earith, C. F. Tebbutt, 1941.

HMV Records and S.I.A.E. Discs.

Houghton and Wyton, Dickinson.

Houghton Mill, The National Trust, 1992.

Inland Waterways of Great Britain, J. Cumberlidge, Imray, 1998.

Legends of the Fenland People, C. Marlowe, Palmer, 1926.

Liable to Floods, J. R. Ravensdale, Camb. Univ. Press, 1974.

Lord Orford's Voyage Around the Fens, Intr. H. J. K. Jenkins, Cambs Library Publs, 1987.

Norfolk, A. Mee, Hodder and Stoughton, 1940.

Norfolk, W. Harrod and C. L. S. Linnell, Faber, 1969.

Norfolk Churches, H. M. Cautley, Allard, 1949.

Norfolk Villages, D. H. Kennett, Hale, 1980.

Northamptonshire, W. Dry, Methuen, 1906.

Northamptonshire, A. Mee, Hodder and Stoughton, 1975.

Northamptonshire and the Soke of Peterborough, J. Smith, Faber and Faber, 1972.

Old Houses and Village Buildings in East Anglia, B. Oliver, Batsford, 1912.

Oxford, C. Hobhouse, Batsford, 1939.

Place Names of Bedfordshire and Huntingdonshire, A. Mawer and F. Stenton, Cambridge, 1926.

Portrait of Bedfordshire, D. H. Kennett, Hale, 1978.

Portrait of Buckinghamshire, J. Camp, Hale, 1972.

Portrait of Cambridgeshire, S. A. Manning, Hale, 1978.

Portrait of the Fen Country, E. Storey, Hale, 1972.

Portrait of Norfolk, D. Yaxley, Hale, 1977.

Rivers of East Anglia, J. Turner, Cassell, 1954.

Roman Britain and Early England, P. Hunter Blair, Sphere Books, 1975.

St Neots Past, R. Young, Phillimore, 1996.

St Ives Official Guide. R. Burn-Murdoch, Local Authority
Publishing Co. Ltd.

St Ives, Slepe by the Ouse. N. Hudson, St Ives Town Council, 1989.

Suffolk and Norfolk, M. R. James, Dent, 1930.

The Ancient Bridges of East and Mid England, E. Jervoise,
The Architectural Press, 1932.

The Anglo Saxon Chronicles, Trl. G. N. Garmonsway, Dent, 1953.

The Black Fens, A. K. Astbury, EP Publishing, 1973.

The Book of Huntingdon, C. Dunn, Hollen Street Press,1990.

The Brewers of Cromwell's Country, K. Osborn, Osborn, 1999.

The Buildings of Bedfordshire, and the County of Huntingdon
and Peterborough, N. Pevsner, Penguin Books, 1974.

The Buildings of England, Buckinghamshire, N. Pevsner, Penguin,
1973.

The Buildings of England, Cambridgeshire, N. Pevsner, Penguin, 1954.

The Buildings of England, North West and South Norfolk, N. Pevsner,
Penguin, 1962.

The Cambridge, Ely and King's Lynn Road, C. G. Harper, Chapman
and Hall, 1902.

The Cambridgeshire Landscape, C. Taylor, Hodder and Stoughton,
1973.

The Changing Fenland, H. C. Darby, Camb. Univ. Press, 1974.

The Concise Dictionary of National Biography, Oxford, 1992.

The Concise Oxford Dictionary of English Place Names, E. Ekwall,
Oxford, 1976.

The Draining of the Fens, H. C. Darby, Camb. Univ. Press, 1940.

The Fenland Past and Present, S. H. Miller and S. B. J. Skertchley,
Longmans, 1878.

The Fens, A. Bloom, Robert Hale, 1953.

The Great Level, D. Summers, David and Charles, 1976.

The Great Ouse, D. Summers, David and Charles, 1973.

The Manor, Hemingford Grey, Brochure.

The Medieval Fenland, H. C. Darby, David and Charles, 1974.

The Middle Level, A. Hunter Blair, Imray Laurie Norie and Wilson,
2000.

The Old Ferry Boat Inn, Brochure.

The Origins of Norfolk, T. Williamson, Manchester Univ. Press, 1993.

The Ouse, A. J. Foster, SPCK.

The Pathfinder Station. S. Peach, JMS Design, St Ives, 1983.

The Pike and Eel Hotel, Brochure.

The River Great Ouse and Tributaries, A. Hunter Blair, Imray Laurie
Norie and Wilson, 2000.

The Shell Guide to England, Ed. J. Hadfield, Michael Joseph, 1970.
The Skaters of the Fens, A. Bloom, Heffer, 1958.
The Three Jolly Butchers, Brochure.
Vermuyden and the Fens, L. E Harris, Cleaver Hume, 1953.

Ordnance Survey Explorer Maps:
    191 Banbury, Bicester and Chipping Norton
    192 Buckingham and Milton Keynes
    207 Newport Pagnell and Northampton South
    208 Bedford and St Neots
    225 Huntingdon and St Ives
    228 March and Ely
    236 King's Lynn, Downham Market and Swaffham.